A Commonsense Guide to

BILINGUAL EDUCATION

Judith Lessow-Hurley

Association for Supervision and Curriculum Development   Alexandria, Virginia

The Author

Judith Lessow-Hurley is Associate Professor of Education at San José State University, San José, California.

ASCD publications present a variety of viewpoints. The views expressed or implied in this publication should not be interpreted as official positions of the Association.

Printed in the United States of America by Automated Graphics Systems.

Cover design by Karen Monaco

Ronald S. Brandt, *Executive Director*
Nancy Modrak, *Managing Editor, Books and Editorial Services*
Julie Houtz, *Senior Associate Editor*
Cole Tucker, *Editorial Assistant*
Gary Bloom, *Manager, Design and Production Services*
Karen Monaco, *Senior Graphic Designer*
Valerie Sprague, *Desktop Publisher*

$6.95
ASCD Stock Number: 611-91115

Library of Congress Cataloging-in-Publication Data
Lessow-Hurley, Judith.
 A commonsense guide to bilingual education / Judith Lessow-Hurley.
  p.   cm.
 Includes bibliographical references.
 ISBN 0-87120-183-6
 1. Education, Bilingual—United States.   I. Title.
LC3731.L47   1991
371.97′ 00973—dc20

91-21874
CIP

A Commonsense Guide to

BILINGUAL EDUCATION

Introduction

S ay to any group of professional educators: "Raise your hands if you took two or more years of a foreign language in high school or college," and invariably all hands will come up. Continue with the question "How many of you feel you are proficient in that language?" and hands are quickly lowered. If your next question is "How many of you wish you spoke a second language?" you'll once again see all hands in the air.

Most of us think it would be useful, even prestigious, to be bilingual. Educators, especially, recognize the ability to speak more than one language as the hallmark of an educated person. Even so, when asked whether they favor bilingual instructional programs, educators usually say, "No, I don't." What accounts for this discrepancy in our attitudes about bilingualism in general and bilingual education in particular?

In the last twenty years bilingual education has become highly politicized. Emotionally charged debates have clouded many essential issues and set the stage for the dissemination of inaccurate information. Lack of support and shortages of resources have led to bare-bones programs that often do not display the characteristics of exemplary dual-language instruction.

The brief discussion in this book is intended to:

• Set the record straight on bilingual programs through a careful analysis of issues,

• Provide professional educators with a working, up-to-date knowledge of research,

• Offer professional educators the opportunity to explore innovative and exemplary formats for dual-language programming, and

• Broaden professional thinking on bilingual education to include programs for both limited-English-proficient students and monolingual native English speakers (anglophones).

Chapter 1 provides an overview of language policy, because language policy is part of the political environment within which we must consider bilingual education. Chapter 2 focuses on language proficiency assessment. Chapter 3 discusses bilingual program models and Chapter 4 presents methods of instruction used in bilingual classrooms. Chapter 5 describes the roles of teachers and paraprofessionals in bilingual classrooms. Chapter 6 analyzes legal issues and clarifies requirements for serving limited-English-proficient children. Chapter 7 answers questions frequently asked about bilingual education. Each chapter includes several suggested sources for readers who want to pursue issues in greater depth.

Increasingly, educators must consider ways to effectively educate students who may not have sufficient English to succeed in English-only classrooms. In addition, we must try to address the issues of a global economy and a shrinking world. Bilingual education offers possibilities for meeting both those challenges. Many professional sources and indexes list "bilingual education" as a subcategory of "compensatory education." That's unfortunate—bilingual education offers worthwhile opportunities for all students.

1

Language Policy and Bilingual Education: An Overview

Language Use and Policy Around the World

L anguage use around the world is extremely complex. Francois Grosjean, in his book *Life With Two Languages* (1982), suggests there are only two nations in the world that might be considered monolingual: Japan and what was then West Germany. He notes, however, that Japan's inhabitants, although overwhelmingly of Japanese ethnic origin, also include indigenous Ainu, as well as Korean and Chinese minorities who maintain their ethnic languages in addition to speaking Japanese. Likewise, the German population includes immigrant workers from Turkey, Yugoslavia, Italy, and Greece. So even these two seemingly monolingual nations are marked by linguistic diversity.

In other countries, numerous languages are used daily, but one language is declared the "official" language. This is common where colonies have gained independence and adopted a colonial language to facilitate national unity across ethnic groups. Colonial languages are widely understood, and selecting a European language avoids the appearance of favoring one ethnic group over others. In Nigeria, for example, English is the official language, although some 250 languages are spoken there. Many ethnically diverse nations in Africa have chosen English or French as their official language; others, like Tanzania, have chosen Swahili. Swahili is a lingua franca in Africa, but unlike English and French, it has no colonial overtones.

Some countries have more than one official language. Switzerland is officially trilingual in German, Italian, and French, and a fourth language, Romansch, is considered a national language. Many countries have two official languages, including Canada (English and French), Belgium (Flemish and French), and Israel (Hebrew and Arabic). India, where over 200 languages are spoken, has 14 national languages and recognizes English as official. Hindi is also an official language of India, but Indian Muslims are uneasy about the potential political dominance of Hindus, so Hindi has never been fully accepted by the whole population.

What does it mean for a country to be *officially* bilingual or multilingual? It doesn't mean that all citizens speak all the official languages, nor that they are required to. It does mean that transactions in the official sphere must be conducted in official languages.

Switzerland, for example, is divided into *cantons*, political subdivisions comparable to the states of the United States. Each canton's official language is the language of its majority population. For business at the state level, a person must use the canton language. Any dealings with the federal government, however, can be accomplished in any of the country's three official languages. Not everyone in Switzerland is bilingual; the size of the country promotes significant language contact, but a person need only speak one language to accomplish daily tasks. In multilingual situations, some percentage of the population will inevitably develop proficiency in more than one language, and those individuals generally help others communicate through translation and interpretation.

Language Policy in the United States

The United States is an example of a multilingual country that has no official language policy. English clearly dominates, but many indigenous Native American languages are spoken too. Spanish is indigenous to the Southwest, and Hawaiian Creole to the island state. German and other European languages have their roots in prerevolutionary immigration, and new heritage languages take root every day as immigration continues and the diversity of our newcomers increases.

The framers of the Constitution, facing the linguistic diversity of their time, made an affirmative decision not to select an official language for the United States. The Continental Congress published many documents in German to facilitate communication with the German community, which was active in the Revolution. That is probably the root of the erroneous notion that the nation's founders considered German as a possible official language. Hebrew was considered for official recognition, more as a symbol of piety and scholarship than as an actual tool for government or daily business. Ultimately, though, no official language was specified in the Constitution.

Individual Bilingualism

Statistics are readily available as to the number of languages in the world, and the number of people who speak them, but we have no information on the number of bilingual people in the world. As we will see later, this is partly because the term "bilingual" is not easy to define. As Grosjean points out, "there are from 3,000 to 4,000 languages in the world today . . . and only about 150 countries to house them in" (1982, p. 4). Given the complexities of language use and policy around the world, there can be no doubt that individual bilingualism is common.

Bilingual Education: Historical Perspectives

We tend to think of bilingual education as a new idea. Critics sometimes suggest that it is a modern invention designed for the sole purpose of creating jobs for disenfranchised minorities. But bilingual education is common around the world and has been since antiquity. In ancient Rome, for example, educated people learned both Latin and Greek. While Romans schooled their children in Greek, which was considered the language of erudition and prestige, they promulgated Latin across their empire, and proficiency in Latin was one avenue through which Roman subjects could hope to assimilate, advance, and enjoy the fruits of membership in the prevailing order. Consequently, Latin was the language of schooling in Europe throughout the Middle Ages, until the rise of nationalism and the Protestant Reformation changed perceptions about the value of local languages.

In general, until the development of technology for disseminating written material, all scholars and educated people needed more than one language so that they could read what few printed materials were available.

Bilingual Education Today: The Canadian Example

Political and linguistic realities combined result in bilingual education programs all around the world. Educators in the United States need not look far, however, to see successful approaches to dual-language instruction. Canada has taken an assertive stance in the area of language policy, using immersion education as a planning tool for enhancing the status of French and promoting positive intergroup relations between anglophones (English speakers) and francophones (French speakers). Immersion education is a form of dual-language instruction that uses a second language as the medium of instruction, in an environment carefully controlled so that students can understand what is being taught and make their needs known.

In 1965, a community of anglophone parents in Quebec supported the establishment of a French immersion program for their children. The St. Lambert experiment, as it is often called, was extremely successful. Children developed a reasonable level of proficiency in French, were successful in their subjects, and also developed positive attitudes about French Canadian culture and French speakers (Genesee 1987). Immersion models were replicated all over Canada, and have captured the attention of educators in the United States.

The success of Canadian immersion programs is tied to several important factors, including program design, the socioeconomic status of the students, and the status of the target language. Immersion programs do not work everywhere for everyone, and they should not be confused with *submersion* programs, where children are simply placed in classrooms in which the language of instruction differs from their own. (The immersion model is discussed in detail in Chapter 3.)

Part of the rationale for the Canadian programs has been the desire to foster positive social and political relations between the English-speaking majority and the French-speaking minority. To some extent, Canada's language and education policies have promoted improved relations. Language acceptance, however, may be only a manifestation of deeper social and political currents. Fueled by confidence in their developing economies, the French-speaking provinces are once again considering independence.

Canada, like many industrialized nations, has a high rate of immigration from less-developed countries, so many languages besides French and English are spoken. As yet, the country has no clear language policy regarding the role of what Canadians call the "heritage languages" of its newcomers.

Bilingual Education in the United States

The United States has been characterized by linguistic diversity since before its inception as a nation. Although English was the primary language of the thirteen colonies, German, French, Dutch, and other European languages had a significant presence in the United States in the 18th and 19th centuries. Spanish was indigenous to what is now the southwestern United States, and a multitude of Native American languages, only a few of which remain today, were spoken across the continent. Bilingual education, too, has existed since the country's earliest times.

The German Example

Starting before the American Revolution and continuing well into the 19th century, instruction in German was widespread. The use of German was tolerated for several reasons. First, the Germans were widely and highly regarded as patriots because they had fought on the side of the Revolution. Second, they settled primarily in the Midwest, which during that period was still relatively remote from the eastern centers of population and power. Their relative isolation, combined with their geographical concentration and political sophistication, allowed the Germans to organize their communities as they saw fit.

The 19th century witnessed the growth of urban centers and the centralization of school administration. Schooling was not compulsory in most places, however, and to attract children, public schools had to compete with parochial school offerings and comply with community demands.

St. Louis was one of the first cities in the nation to establish a large centralized school district, and German instruction was an important part of the curriculum. By 1880, fifty-two of the fifty-seven public schools in St. Louis had German-language programs, serving not only German-speaking children but also English-speaking children who learned German as a second language (Escamilla 1980).

Other Languages

Although German was prevalent, it was not the only language served by dual-language programs in the 19th century. Some form of bilingual education was available in Spanish, French, Czech, Polish, Italian, Dutch, Swedish, Norwegian, and Danish (Ovando and Collier 1985). In addition to the languages of European immigrants, many Native American languages were spoken across the continent. Insofar as the federal government allowed local control of education, many Native Americans were educated in their indigenous language as well as in English. The Cherokees, for example, maintained a large system of formal bilingual schooling (Castellanos 1983).

Nativist Reactions

Intense immigration in the 19th century provoked a nativist reaction not unlike the anti-immigration and English-only movements of today. Anti-immigrationist sentiment was primarily directed at the Irish, who arrived in large numbers in the northeastern states in the mid-1800s. Poor, illiterate, and Catholic, the Irish were widely hated and feared. A few vocal protestants portrayed Catholics as loyal to a foreign pope and claimed that affording them the rights of citizens would effectively bring the United States under the dominion of the Catholic church.

Since much of the German community was also Catholic, anti-Catholic sentiments found a clearly defined target in the German language. Soon, foreign allegiance became associated with foreign languages. Across the Midwest, laws were passed to prevent the use of German in public schools and, when the German community retrenched to its parochial schools, in private schools as well. The politically sophisticated German community was quick to respond and used their votes to resist the onslaught of legislation restricting the use of their language.

Sentiment, however, is difficult to control, and as World War I neared, anti-German feeling increased. Programs disassembled by legislation were never reassembled, as teachers and students scattered and parents became increasingly disinclined to publicly affirm their ethnic identity. The nativist movements of the 19th century had their way—German was never again to flourish in the United States as it had before the turn of the century.

World War II and Beyond

World War II was a catalyst for language instruction in the United States. The military, faced with an urgent need for speakers of a variety of languages, turned its attention to developing fast and effective second-language teaching techniques. The audio-lingual approach, then a radical departure from traditional teaching methodologies, was developed by the United States Army. Following World War II, Congress passed the National Defense Education Act (1958), which provided funding for foreign language study, affording language ability its rightful place in national defense.

World War II also provided a backdrop for the civil rights movement, which in turn had a dynamic effect on the rights of minorities to preserve their native language. Many African Americans and Mexican Americans fought in the war. Beyond the borders of their hometowns, they discovered a world where multilingualism was normal and color did not affect their status as liberators. Many soldiers of ethnic minority gave their lives in World War II, and the returning survivors were unwilling to bear the burden of segregation, to tolerate the assertion that they were less than American.

As the civil rights movement gained momentum, cultural pluralism took on real meaning as a model for American society, and Americans began to assert their ethnic identity. Language identification was an important part of ethnic identity.

The Cuban Revolution in 1959 resulted in an influx of Cubans to Florida, which in turn spurred the creation of the first large-scale bilingual education program since World War II—at the Coral Way School in Dade County, Florida, in 1963. The program was successful for complex political reasons. Cuban refugees were upper-class, highly educated, and politically sophisticated. Light-skinned and cosmopolitan, they were readily accepted into United States society. The federal government was eager to support their anti-communist and anti-Castro agendas and provided extensive funding for the Coral Way program. The program was also substantially supplemented by private-sector funds. Given the nature of the Cuban refugee population, staffing the program with skilled teachers was not difficult.

The political climate of the post-war period, combined with the success of the Coral Way program, led to government policy favoring the establishment of bilingual programs:

• *Title VII of the Elementary and Secondary Education Act (ESEA).* In 1968 President Lyndon B. Johnson signed the ESEA into law. Title VII of that Act, known as the Bilingual Education Act, provided discretionary funding for model programs that used non-English-language instruction to assist children academically while they mastered the English language. The act has been amended several times over the last twenty-two years. In its present form, Title VII supports basic instructional programs, teacher training, graduate education, research, and the dissemination of materials for use in bilingual classrooms.

• *Lau v. Nichols, 414 U.S. 563 (1974).* In 1974, the United States Supreme Court found for the plaintiffs in *Lau v. Nichols.* Basing their case on Title VI of the Civil Rights Act, a group of Chinese students sued the San Francisco Unified School District. The Court decided the district had violated the students' civil rights by providing them with an education in a language they could not understand. Subsequent legislation and court decisions have supplanted *Lau* as the basis for the asserting the rights of language-minority students. The decision, however, represents a landmark in the field of bilingual education. (Current legal issues are discussed in Chapter 6.)

The Politics of Bilingualism

The emotional quality of the debate surrounding bilingual education in the United States is rooted to some extent in our attitudes about language and about bilingualism. As a nation, we exhibit several forms of language resistance, which can be classified into three tendencies: Language parochialism, language elitism, and language restrictionism (Lessow-Hurley 1990).

Language Parochialism

Americans generally feel that everyone ought to speak English, and they are reinforced in that notion by the fact that many people actually do. In the last century, English has become the dominant language of politics, science, commerce, and education all around the world. While we have come to expect that airline attendants and shopkeepers will oblige our monolingualism, our language parochialism has been costly for us, both in world trade and in national defense.

Global markets and interdependent economies require that we maximize our ability to speak to people around the world. We may be competing with them, selling to them, or learning from them. The American business community is slowly recognizing that it pays to be linguistically and culturally sophisticated in a shrinking world. No one wants to repeat the classic mistake committed by General Motors in its marketing of the Nova automobile in Latin America (Simon 1980): To Spanish speakers "Chevy Nova" means "Chevy doesn't go"—not good advertising at all.

Errors like that may be amusing, but they are also costly. Even more costly is our inability to receive and process information necessary for the national defense. One source reports that only one in five CIA officers stationed in Mexico City can speak Spanish (Harper's Index 1990). We have enormous language wealth in the United States, but situations like those just described show that we are starving in the midst of plenty. History teaches us the benefit of using our language resources wisely. During World War II, the army relied on the Navajo Code Talkers, native Navajo speakers, to transmit classified information. Navajo was the only code that Japanese code breakers were unable to decipher. Ironically, although the Code Talkers were decorated as heroes of the war, government policy had suppressed the use of Native American languages for over a century.

Language Elitism

Language elitism is the commonly held attitude that bilingualism is acceptable only for members of the upper class. We tend to believe that speaking more than one language is cultured if the individual who speaks it learned the language in school. We tend to believe that French and German are more prestigious than Spanish, despite its being, arguably, an indigenous American language and, inarguably, widely spoken in the United States.

Many expensive private schools include second-language instruction as a part of the basic curriculum. The French for Tots program in New York City, for example, at one point had 152 one-year-olds on its waiting list (Harper's Index 1990, p. 17). Clearly, we promote bilingualism for a small, elite sector of the population. When presented with language-minority students, however, we ask them to forget their first language and supplant it with English. In so doing we squander our linguistic wealth, acting on unexamined and counterproductive biases. We would do well to consider second-language instruction for everyone: English as a second language for limited-English-proficient students, and enrichment languages for monolingual English speakers.

Language Restrictionism

Governments can suppress or support languages, and in so doing also engineer broad social goals. The Canadian example described earlier showed how government policy on language and bilingual instruction can be used to further positive intergroup relations. On the other hand, the Soviet Union has suppressed the use of local languages in Estonia, Latvia, Lithuania, and its other federated states in an attempt to eliminate ethnic nationalism. Independence movements in those areas have been accompanied by demands for language recognition.

In the United States, we have recently become focused on narrow and nativist goals. Overwhelmed by increases in immigration and disconcerted by the diversity of our newcomers, we have fallen back on the 19th century strategy of mandating the use of English in the public sphere. Proponents of English-only legislation have targeted two areas:

• *Bilingual voting.* English-only proponents charge that bilingual ballots are costly and discourage people from learning English. But bilingual ballots are protected by the Voting Rights Act of 1965 and are only required in carefully defined and limited situations. They are not costly and encourage participation in the political system, which in turn promotes involvement in all aspects of American life.

• *Bilingual schooling.* English-only proponents suggest that children should spend no more than three years in transitional programs where the home language is used for academic support. But research shows that full development of a first language supports the acquisition of a second. In addition, children require five to seven years of second-language development before they can function at their academic level in the new language. (A rationale for primary-language instruction is outlined in Chapter 3.)

My Grandfather Learned English—Why Can't They?

In the past, many immigrants gave up their first language as part of the process of becoming "Americanized." You may wonder, then, why the situation should be different today. The response is clear:

• Although our grandparents learned English, they learned it only well enough to survive in an economy driven by labor. Today's work world is based far more on service, and it requires far greater language proficiency than our grandparents' world.

• As this book outlines in Chapter 3, proficiency in two languages gives students an academic advantage. Language is the basic instrument of schooling. Students who work well with two sets of tools are better prepared than those who work well with only one.

• Forcing children to struggle in school settings where they cannot understand or be understood is cruel. People have survived that system, but in this, as in all other areas, we continue to strive for humane solutions to the challenges students face.

• Our parochialism, elitism, and restrictionism are costly. In a shrinking world and a global economy, proficiency in more than one language is a plus.

Read More About . . .

• Language policy and bilingualism around the world in *Life with Two Languages: An Introduction to Bilingualism*, by Francois Grosjean (Cambridge: Harvard University Press, 1982).

• Language policy in the United States in *The English-Only Question: An Official Language for Americans*, by Dennis Baron (New Haven: Yale University Press, 1990), and *Only English? Law and Language Policy in the United States*, by Bill Piatt (Albuquerque: University of New Mexico Press, 1990).

• Historical perspectives on bilingual education, the politics of the English-only movement, and other related issues in *Bilingual Education: History, Politics, Theory, and Practice*, by James Crawford (Trenton: Crane, 1989).

2

Who Is the Limited-English-Proficient Student?

Basic Definitions

Language-Minority Students

L anguage-minority students have a language other than English in their home background. A language-minority student may share a household with, for example, a parent or grandparent who speaks a language other than English. On the other hand, a language-minority student may come from a home where English is rarely or never spoken. A language-minority child may be bilingual, limited-English-proficient (LEP), or English monolingual.

School districts usually identify language-minority students as a first step to identifying LEP students. Home language surveys are one way to identify language-minority students. The home language surveys used in many California districts ask the following questions:

• Which language did your son or daughter learn when he or she first learned to talk?

• What language does your son or daughter most frequently use at home?

• What language do you use most frequently to speak to your son or daughter?

• Name the language most often spoken by the adults at home.

Although the exact number of language-minority students in the United States is unknown, it is clearly growing, and in some districts with large immigrant populations it has exceeded 50 percent of the school population. Once a school district has identified a student as a language minority, it can determine whether the student is LEP and make appropriate placement decisions.

LEP Students

LEP students are those who, by some measure, have insufficient English to succeed in English-only classrooms. Emphasis must be placed on the phrase "by some measure." Definitions of the term "limited-English-proficient" and the measures used to assess proficiency vary widely from district to district, and lack of uniformity in assessment is a significant problem both in identifying the needs of LEP students and in meeting those needs. No one knows exactly how many LEP students there are in the United States; recent estimates range from 3.5 million to 5.3 million in kindergarten through 6th grade (Ambert 1988).

What Is Language Proficiency?

One of the difficulties in identifying LEP students is the lack of agreement among theorists on a definition of proficiency. Some theorists suggest that a single factor underlies language proficiency. More widely accepted, though, is the theory that language proficiency involves a number of separate abilities. If that is the case, each language ability should be tested separately, since it is possible for a person's level of proficiency to vary across different language skills. For example, a person may read and write a second language well, but lack fluency in speaking.

Language Use and Context

Attempts to define proficiency have led to the idea that it is context related. For example, if you have studied French extensively in college, you may be capable of writing essays in French on topics related to literature or philosophy. Stepping off a plane at Orly, however, you may find that your French is insufficient to the demands of changing money, finding a bus to Paris, or registering at your hotel. It's not that you don't know any French, but that you are stronger in some language skills than in others. The converse also applies. For example, many Americans are native speakers of Spanish. In the absence of academic support for their native language, however, they may lack Spanish literacy skills. Their oral proficiency is perfectly adequate for the requirements of daily life, such as shopping, phone calls, and social events, but they might have difficulty writing a formal academic paper in Spanish.

Understanding the notion of context-related proficiency brings us closer to an understanding of bilingualism. Very few speakers of more than one language are balanced bilinguals. That is, very few people command a full repertoire of communicative skills in two languages, because most people are rarely called upon to use both their languages in every situation. It is far more common for bilingual people to use one language in some domains and the second language in others.

Communicative competence is the ability to use language to negotiate the many different situations a person encounters in real life. According to a widely accepted model of communicative competence developed by Canale and Swain (1980), proficient speakers of a language have:

- *Grammatical competence*—mastery of the sound system, vocabulary, and syntax of a language.
- *Sociolinguistic competence*—an understanding of what is appropriate to say, based on the relationships of the speakers, the setting, the function of the interaction, and other social conditions.
- *Discourse competence*—the ability to understand a series of sentences and to produce series that are coherent and appropriate.
- *Strategic competence*—the ability to overcome failures in communication, for example, by asking speakers to repeat or clarify what they have said, or to speak more slowly.

It is clear from the Canale and Swain model of communicative competence that an understanding of context and the use of language appropriate to a particular context are important to proficiency.

Implications for Schooling

The role of context in language proficiency has come to the fore in recent thinking about the identification of LEP students. Cummins (1981) has suggested that school-related tasks require school-related proficiency, which he labeled Cognitive Academic Language Proficiency (CALP). Recently, educators have begun to use the term "empowering language" to describe this sophisticated kind of language required in classroom settings (California State Department of Education 1990). CALP differs from Basic Interpersonal Communicative Skills (BICS), sometimes called "functional language"—the language skills we use for everyday tasks.

According to Cummins (1981), tasks in school are often context-reduced, or lacking in the clues that promote understanding in day-to-day situations, such as tone of voice, gesture, facial expression, concrete objects, and shared assumptions. School-related, context-reduced tasks present difficulties to students lacking cognitive academic language proficiency.

Educators who are not trained in second-language acquisition may evaluate language proficiency based on students' performance in informal situations. Students who seem proficient in English in the schoolyard, however, may lack the language skills necessary to function in the classroom. Cummins' framework for language proficiency is significant because it points out the special requirements of classroom situations. We can quickly understand the demands placed on LEP students in English-only classrooms if we ask ourselves this question: How well would I need to know Spanish (or any new language) to function in a classroom at my current academic level, in competition with native speakers?

How Do Schools Test Language Proficiency?

Given that language proficiency has many facets and that it is related to specific contexts or situations, testing language proficiency is difficult. Proficiency measures often assess the ability to manage subsystems of language: phonology (the sound system), morphology (parts of words, like plural markers, tense markers, prefixes), syntax (the structure of language), or semantics (meanings). Such tests are called "discrete point" tests, because they scrutinize separately each subsystem of language. They do not, however, provide a true measure of communicative competence.

For example, a person may have a near-native accent, but limited understanding of meanings and idiomatic phrases. On the other hand, a person with a noticeably non-native accent may be quite proficient in a broad spectrum of social and professional situations. We tend to think of accent as an important component of language proficiency, but there is a wide range of deviations from native phonology, and it is possible to be quite proficient in a second language and still have a "foreign" accent.

Spontaneous language samples scored globally by trained examiners produce reasonably valid measures of communicative competence. Such tests, however, are difficult to formulate and expensive to administer to large numbers of students. Two language proficiency tests frequently used in public schools are:

• The Bilingual Syntax Measure (BSM) I and II by M. K. Burt, H. C. Dulay, and E. Hernandez-Chavez (New York: The Psychological Corporation, 1976). The BSM is designed to measure mastery of syntax structures, on the assumption that syntax development is a measure of second-language acquisition. The test is administered to children individually. The examiner attempts to elicit a sample of natural, spontaneous language by asking a series of questions about pictures in a booklet and recording the child's responses. Responses are scored for grammatical correctness, and language proficiency is reported on a scale ranging from Level 1 (No English) to Level 5 (Proficient English). The BSM is available in Spanish and can be used for comparing a bilingual child's relative proficiency in both languages (i.e., determining language dominance).

• Language Assessment Scales (LAS) by E. De Avila and S. Duncan (Monterey, Calif.: CTB, Macmillan/McGraw-Hill, 1990). PRE-LAS assesses the oral language skills of kindergarten and 1st grade students. LAS-O assesses the oral language skills of students in grades 1 through 12. A new test, LAS R/W, assesses the reading and writing skills of students in grades 2 through 12. LAS test scores are reported along a scale of five levels. The tests are available in Spanish.

LAS oral tests assess students' ability to distinguish between phonemes, produce phonemes, understand the meaning of individual words and whole sentences, and retell a story demonstrating comprehension. The reading and writing component tests vocabulary, comprehension, mechanics, and comprehension. Oral components are administered individually. The reading and writing test can be administered to a group.

Issues in Language Proficiency Testing

School personnel must be aware of areas of concern in language proficiency testing. As mentioned earlier, lack of uniformity in measuring language proficiency may lead to confusion in the field and may also affect our perception of the number of children who need special assistance in our schools. In addition to this broad concern, we must consider other issues:

• *Test administration: the test takers.* As anyone who works with children knows, even the most verbal child may become uncommunicative in a one-to-one testing situation. Because language proficiency assessment rests heavily on language performance, children who are intimidated by testing situations may be incorrectly assessed. This is particularly true for language-minority children who may not be from the cultural mainstream, and who may be especially uncomfortable in traditional testing situations.

• *Test administration: the test givers.* English proficiency tests are best administered by native English speakers. Given the demographics of school personnel, such test administrators are usually middle-class teachers of European descent. Minority students' performance may be affected by teachers' subtle biases or by their body language, eye contact patterns, voice cues, and other features of communication styles. Because bilingual teachers are in short supply, assessments in languages other than English are often administered by paraprofessionals or community volunteers. Such people may be proficient in non-English languages and highly motivated, but they may not be as conversant with testing issues as trained professional teachers.

• *Test construction: validity.* Assessment instruments must be valid—that is, they must test what they purport to test. Language proficiency testing in schools generally involves tests that address discrete subsystems of language; they may not provide an adequate measure of a child's ability to function in an English-only academic environment.

• *Test construction: reliability.* Test results must be consistent regardless of who administers the test or when it is given. In language proficiency testing, reliability is tied to the length of the test (Clark and Lett 1988). Testing in school settings is often constrained by time, and popular tests do not allow for extended sampling of spontaneous speech.

• *Practical considerations.* School districts are often short of time, money, and trained personnel. Given this reality, as well as the issues discussed above, school personnel need to consider global assessments that take into account not only the results of standardized tests, but also observations made by parents and teachers.

Read More About . . .

• Language assessment in *Communication Assessment of the Bilingual Bicultural Child,* edited by J. G. Erickson and D. R. Omark (Baltimore: University Park Press, 1981).

• Language proficiency tests in *Reviews of English Language Proficiency Tests,* edited by J. Charles Alderson, Karl J. Krahnake, and Charles W. Stansfield (Washington, D.C.: Teachers of English to Speakers of Other Languages, 1987).

• Bias in testing and other assessment-related issues in *Bilingualism and Special Education: Issues in Assessment and Pedagogy,* by Jim Cummins (San Diego: College-Hill Press, 1984).

• The distinction between cognitive academic language proficiency and basic interpersonal communication skills in *Schooling and Language Minority Students: A Theoretical Framework,* edited by the California State Department of Education Office of Bilingual Bicultural Education (Los Angeles: CSU-LA Evaluation, Dissemination and Assessment Center, 1981). In particular, see the chapter by Jim Cummins, "The Role of Primary Language Development in Promoting Academic Success for Language Minority Students."

3

Bilingual Program Models

An Education in Two Languages

Misinformation about bilingual education often stems from misunderstandings about program models and methods used within particular models. Let's begin with the assumption that bilingual programs are those that use two languages in some format for instructional purposes. Within that broad framework there are many possible variations.

Primary-Language Instruction

Few people, when questioned directly, deny the value of knowing two languages. "I studied French in high school," people say with a sigh, "and now I can't speak a word. I really wish I could speak a second language." Given the prevalence of that attitude, it's surprising that many people find bilingual education controversial, and resist the idea of using languages other than English in public school classrooms. "Why should I use my tax dollars," the argument goes, "to teach these kids a foreign language? They should learn English as quickly as possible, and we should expose them to English as much as we can." The resistance to bilingual education is actually a resistance to the use of languages other than English for instruction in the public schools.

The argument against the use of primary-language instruction sounds powerful and has strong intuitive appeal, but it breaks down under careful scrutiny. Contrary to popular belief, research indicates that primary-language instruction in the classroom helps students learn English and fosters academic success:

• *Concepts and skills that students learn in one language transfer to another.* Time spent learning in a language other than English is not time wasted. In fact, for many children, time spent in their primary language is time gained on academic tasks (Aldemir 1989).

Consider the LEP child who enters kindergarten in an English-only classroom. By the end of the year, that child may have developed some command of English. But while that child is attempting to decipher the language code, all the other children in class are learning the kindergarten curriculum. In a primary-language instructional setting, LEP students can learn appropriate skills and concepts without falling behind their English-speaking peers.

• *Strong primary-language development helps students learn English.* At first, this point may appear illogical, but in fact, it makes good sense: Students who understand how their native language works can transfer their understanding to their study of English as a second language. According to one study, LEP students who entered English-as-a-second-language (ESL) programs between the ages of 8 and 11 were faster achievers than LEP students who entered ESL programs between the ages of 5 and 7 (Collier and Thomas 1987). Cognitive and linguistic maturity seems to give older students an advantage over younger ones, who have a limited understanding of the workings of the world and of their language.

• *Students need five to seven years to develop cognitive academic language proficiency (CALP)* (Cummins 1981, Miller 1990). School-related tasks require a fairly sophisticated grasp of language. Even after LEP students can manage day-to-day situations in a new language, they may experience difficulty in meeting the academic expectations of an English-only classroom. Primary-language instruction gives those students time to develop CALP without losing important academic ground.

• *Students who are highly proficient in two languages do better academically than monolingual students.* Classroom instruction revolves around language. Bilingual students who have access to more than one language code appear to have the academic advantage of highly developed metalinguistic and problem-solving skills (Baker 1988, Cummins and Swain 1986).

• *Supporting the primary language bolsters self-esteem.* Language is an inseparable part of an individual's personal and cultural identity. To the extent that the school validates a child's language (and by extension, culture), that child will feel valued in the classroom (Baker 1988). In addition, support for community languages transmits a welcoming and empowering message to parents and encourages them to become involved in their children's education (Miller 1990).

Additive versus Subtractive Bilingualism

We can begin to resolve the debate over the value of primary-language instruction for LEP students by learning about the difference between subtractive bilingualism and additive bilingualism.

A subtractive bilingual is a person who has replaced a first language with a new one; the first language is undeveloped, or lost. Students become subtractive bilinguals when schools do not support primary-language development. Such students may maintain oral proficiency in their primary language, but they don't enjoy the benefits of language and literacy development for that language. Compared with additive bilinguals, subtractive bilinguals are at an academic disadvantage.

An additive bilingual is a person who has learned a second language in addition to his native language. Monolingual English-speaking students become additive bilinguals when they acquire a second language. LEP students can become additive bilinguals in programs that maintain their first language and add English as a second language. Additive bilinguals seem to have an academic advantage over subtractive bilinguals and monolinguals.

Understanding the difference between additive and subtractive bilingualism, and the value of additive bilingualism, clarifies the need for both second-language instruction for students who speak only English and primary-language instruction for students whose native language is not English.

Program Models

W e began this chapter with the assumption that bilingual education refers to any instructional program that uses two languages. Although this definition is useful for clearing away confusion and political tension, it is an oversimplification that does not provide any analysis of instructional delivery systems. An education in two languages can be delivered in a variety of formats, which can be readily described in terms of the population they serve and their educational goals, as outlined in Figure 3.1.

FIGURE 3.1
Bilingual Program Models

Model	Students Served	Language Goal	Outcome
Transitional	LEP students	English proficiency and English literacy	Subtractive
Maintenance	LEP students	Bilingualism and biliteracy	Additive
Enrichment	Monolingual English speakers	Bilingualism and biliteracy	Additive
Two-way (Developmental)	LEP students and Monolingual English speakers	Bilingualism and biliteracy	Additive

Immersion—See Figure 3.2 on page 27.

Transitional Programs

Transitional programs provide primary-language assistance for LEP students, but the goal of a transitional program is to make students monolingual and monoliterate in English. When the students have gained proficiency in English, they enter English-only classrooms. LEP students in transitional programs have more success in school than those who have no primary-language support. But transitional programs are not additive and do not have the benefits of programs that develop a child's first language as well as English.

Maintenance Programs

Maintenance programs provide English-language and primary-language development for LEP students. The goal of a maintenance program is to make students bilingual and biliterate. Maintenance programs are additive.

Enrichment Programs

Enrichment programs provide dual-language instruction for monolingual English-speaking students. The goal of an enrichment program is to make students bilingual and biliterate. Enrichment programs are additive and differ from maintenance programs only in the student population they serve.

Two-Way Programs

A two-way program (sometimes called a developmental program) is a combination of a maintenance program and an enrichment program. Such programs serve a combined population of limited-English-speaking and monolingual English-speaking students. The goal of a two-way program is to make all students bilingual and biliterate.

Immersion Programs

Immersion programs are truly bilingual because the teacher is bilingual and the goal is to make students bilingual and biliterate. Immersion programs use a second language as the instructional medium. A true traditional immersion program has the following important features:

• *The immersion teacher is bilingual.* Although the teacher delivers instruction in a language that is new to the students, they can express themselves and be understood in their own language.
• *The language used for instruction is carefully modified to improve student understanding.* All instruction is supported by the use of visuals, media, and hands-on approaches.
• *Students receive daily language arts instruction in their primary language.*

Submersion Programs

All too often, LEP students are placed in English-only classrooms that are then described as immersion programs. Placing LEP students in classrooms where the language of instruction is incomprehensible, where they cannot be understood, and where there is no support for their primary language has been more appropriately called a "sink-or-swim" or "submersion" program.

Structured Immersion Programs for LEP Students

The success of traditional immersion programs in Canada and more recently in the United States has led policymakers to consider placing LEP students in English immersion settings. The important difference between this approach, which is usually called structured immersion, and submersion is that structured immersion teachers are bilingual.

The early results of such placements indicate that structured immersion programs are not as successful as traditional programs have been in promoting bilingualism and biliteracy. Immersion programs seem to work best when speakers of a majority language are immersed in a minority language. This is because majority-language speakers are in no danger of losing their primary language, which is supported not only by language arts in a true immersion program, but also by the society as a whole. In other words, immersion programs, like others, work best when their emphasis is additive.

Two-way Immersion Programs

The traditional immersion model has generally been promoted as an enrichment program for anglophone students who want to learn a second language. As we saw above, such traditional programs are particularly effective for that group for sociolinguistic reasons. Recently, there has been an increasing interest in two-way, or "bilingual," immersion programs. Such programs serve both LEP and monolingual English-speaking students.

In a two-way immersion program, all instruction is delivered in a non-English language. Classes are mixed and include monolingual English speakers and speakers of the language of instruction.

Monolingual English speakers receive English language arts instruction for part of each day while LEP students receive ESL instruction.

As students advance through the grades, the amount of English language arts and ESL instruction increases. At about the 3rd grade, two things occur: (1) ESL instruction begins to approximate English language arts instruction, as LEP students develop oral proficiency and begin to develop literacy skills; and (2) the program is expanded to include the delivery of some subjects in English. The instructional goal is to create a classroom where half the instruction is delivered in English and half in another language by the 4th or 5th grade.

Except for the content of their early English language development courses, all students receive the same instructional program. Within that program:

• LEP students experience a maintenance program.

• Monolingual English-speaking students experience an enrichment program.

Additional benefits of the two-way immersion program are:

• Integrated classrooms.

• Crosscultural sharing—LEP students often assist monolingual English speakers, serving as translators.

• Language models for all participants.

• Esteem building for minority students, who perceive their language and culture as valued by the majority culture.

• Bilingualism and biliteracy for all students.

Immersion programs are outlined in Figure 3.2 on page 27.

Programs That Work

Basic research indicates that bilingualism has positive effects on school achievement. For several reasons, however, program evaluation results are often equivocal. Many programs are called bilingual even though they may not have a coherent program rationale and model. Shortages of qualified personnel sometimes result in bilingual programs without bilingual staff. Some programs pull students out of regular classes for special instruction. Some may amount to no program at all and are simply submersion by some other name.

FIGURE 3.2
Immersion Program Models

Model	Students Served	Language Goal	Outcome
Traditional Immersion	Monolingual English speakers	Bilingualism and biliteracy	Additive—However, insufficient exposure to native language models may affect the quality of language outcomes.
English Immersion (Structured)	LEP students	Bilingualism and biliteracy	Subtractive—Program fails to produce additive results because of a lack of societal support for the students' first language.
Two-way Bilingual Immersion	LEP students and monolingual English speakers	Bilingualism and biliteracy	Additive—Functions as a maintenance program for LEP students and a traditional immersion program for mono- lingual English speakers, with added benefits of cross-cultural exchange and language models.
Submersion	LEP students		Subtractive—Submersion = no program.

The California State Department of Education (1990) has summarized the research on effective bilingual programs and lists the following as essential program characteristics:

• Content-based instruction, comparable to material covered in English-only classrooms
• Primary-language instruction for subject matter
• Multicultural instruction that recognizes and incorporates students' home cultures
• Clear goals
• Dedicated administrative and teaching staff with a commitment to bilingual education
• High expectations for all students

• Frequent monitoring of student performance

• Flexibility in instructional approach, which provides students with alternative routes to learning

• Parent and community involvement

• Open communication among all sectors of the school community.

Recent Findings

In February 1991, the United States Department of Education released the results of an extensive longitudinal study conducted in 1984–85 and 1987–88. The study involved 2,000 Spanish-speaking students enrolled in programs in California, Florida, New Jersey, New York, and Texas. Students in the study were enrolled in one of three types of programs:

• *Structured English Immersion.* All instruction in content areas is presented in English, but the teacher is bilingual and uses the native language for clarification.

• *Early-Exit Transitional.* About 30 percent of initial instruction is in the child's native language. Native-language instruction is phased out during 2nd grade and children enter all-English classrooms in 3rd grade.

• *Late-Exit Transitional.* Students are taught in their native language at least 40 percent of the time. Students stay in the program through 6th grade.

Results of the study indicate that LEP students in all three programs achieved better than at-risk students in the general population in reading, mathematics, and language development. Students in structured immersion and early-exit programs, however, lost ground when native-language support was discontinued. Late-exit students, on the other hand, actually gained ground, and appeared to be gaining on students in the general population (United States Department of Education News 1991).

Read More About . . .

• Immersion education in the United States and Canada in *Studies on Immersion Education: A Collection for United States*

Educators, edited by the Office of Bilingual Bicultural Education of the California State Department of Education (Sacramento, 1984). Also see *Learning Through Two Languages: Studies of Immersion and Bilingual Education,* by Fred Genesee (Cambridge: Newbury House, 1987).

• Bilingualism and its effects on achievement in *Bilingualism in Education: Aspects of Theory, Research and Practice,* by Jim Cummins (London: Longman).

• A rationale for primary-language instruction and program models in *The Foundations of Dual Language Instruction,* by Judith Lessow-Hurley (New York: Longman, 1990).

• Programs that work in *On Course: Bilingual Education's Success in California,* by Stephen Krashen and Douglas Biber (California Association for Bilingual Education, 1988).

4

Focus on Instruction

Planning

C ritics of bilingual education are quick to insist that it doesn't work. The "it" they refer to, however, is often not a bilingual *program* at all, but a collection of classrooms that may or may not espouse a consistent philosophy or methodology. In the absence of a coherent program design, good teachers may produce positive outcomes, but they do so against difficult odds in situations that don't maximize chances for success.

In choosing an instructional method, teachers should closely examine the program model. Questions to consider include:

- What are the goals and objectives of the model?
- In keeping with those goals and objectives:
  - What percentage of time should be devoted to first- and second-language development at each grade level? (Depending on the model, this question may apply to LEP students, English monolingual students, or both.)
  - What is the composition of the classroom?
- What resources (human and material) are available?

Ideally, a district will have a master plan that outlines district policy regarding bilingual education, details goals and objectives for instruction for LEP students as well as English monolingual students, and provides some guidance to program directors, site administrators, and teachers who will be implementing the program.

Poor planning or haphazard use of language in the classroom undermines the goals of any program and limits students' opportunities for academic success. Language is an instructional tool, and its use should be an important part of instructional planning in a bilingual classroom. Careful planning of language use can help students learn a language faster and enhance their ability to succeed in an academic setting.

Grouping

ost teachers group for instruction to accommodate learners with different abilities or skill levels. Grouping takes on special meaning in bilingual classrooms, where students have differing levels of ability and of proficiency in a second language. There are two basic approaches to bilingual classroom organization:

• *Linguistically homogeneous groups.* Students are grouped by language dominance. Linguistically homogeneous groups are a requirement where instruction focuses on first-language development and literacy or on second-language instruction. When practical, a teacher may also want to place linguistically homogeneous learners in subgroups based on skill levels and individual needs.

• *Linguistically heterogeneous groups.* Students of different language dominance are in the same group. Linguistically heterogeneous groups are possible for content instruction, but they require special attention to language planning so that all students can understand what is presented.

Examples of linguistically homogeneous and heterogeneous groups are shown in Figure 4.1 on page 33.

Working with Linguistically Heterogeneous Groups

Working with two languages in a linguistically heterogeneous group can be done in several formats:

• *Concurrent translation.* The teacher presents material in both languages in constant alternation. This method may be ineffective for several reasons:

- Teachers tend to favor their stronger language, which is often English, and to overestimate the amount of time they spend delivering instruction in the students' primary language. Often languages other than English are used only for clarifying instructions and managing behavior.
- The task of constantly translating during instruction quickly exhausts even a fully bilingual teacher.
- Students quickly discern that they don't need to pay attention to information presented in their second language, because it will also be available in their first. While they may grasp the material, they lose concomitant opportunities for second-language development.

Concurrent translation is sometimes implemented by a team of teachers or by a teacher and an aide. Working in teams can eliminate the problem of language strength and mitigate the strain of constant translation. The team approach, however, does not eliminate the effect this method may have on student attention. Research indicates that sustained periods of monolingual instruction may be more effective than concurrent translation in promoting the development of two languages (Lindholm 1987).

• *Preview-Review.* The teacher alternates languages within a given lesson:

- A preview is delivered in one of the classroom languages. It generally includes vocabulary development around the essential concepts in the lesson.
- The lesson is delivered in the other classroom language.
- The lesson is reviewed in the same language as the preview. Basic concepts are reinforced, and students have the opportunity to ask and respond to questions that clarify the material presented.

The preview-review method is especially useful for LEP learners when curriculum materials and texts are available only in English. Note that in vocabulary development, teachers should not overlook opportunities to build students' academic language. Textbooks often highlight words related to important new concepts. LEP learners may also need help with words like "list," "analyze," "compare," "outline," and other process vocabulary with which native English speakers may already be familiar.

• *Alternate-day approach.* All instruction except first-language literacy and second-language development alternates from day to day. For example, instruction may be delivered in English on Monday, Spanish on Tuesday, English on Wednesday, and so on. Teachers do not repeat lessons in translation; rather, they continue the curriculum while alternating languages. The preview-review method can dovetail with the alternate-day format. For example, a lesson can be previewed in English on Monday, delivered in Vietnamese on Tuesday, and reviewed in English on Wednesday, in keeping with the alternating format. Teachers using this method should be careful to modify their language use to make material comprehensible to students, and also to recycle skills and concepts throughout the school year to maximize opportunities for students to learn.

FIGURE 4.1
Grouping in Bilingual Classrooms

Linguistically Homogeneous Grouping

Following language proficiency assessment and skill assessment, students are placed in instructional groups. For example, students in a bilingual 3rd grade might be grouped for reading instruction in this way:

Group I: 2.0 level readers, Spanish

Group II: 3.0 level readers, Spanish

Group III: 2.0 level readers, English

Group IV: 3.0 level readers, English

Linguistically Heterogeneous Grouping

Students with different language proficiencies are grouped together for instruction. Heterogeous grouping is inappropriate for reading and language development, but can be used in other content areas. For example, a bilingual 3rd grade might be grouped in this way for mathematics:

Group I: Review of multiplication
             English and Vietnamese speakers

Group II: Introduction of long division
             English and Vietnamese speakers

Cooperative Grouping

Cooperative learning has caught the attention of all educators, because it fosters interpersonal relations, enhances students' problem-solving skills, and increases and upgrades the amount of student-initiated talk in the classroom. Because a cooperative setting increases the amount of subject-related talk among students, it can provide opportunities during content instruction for second-language development in bilingual settings. Teachers who implement cooperative strategies in bilingual classrooms should be aware of two important points:

• Students in cooperative groups are generally allowed to communicate in any language they choose. Nevertheless, cooperative groups tend to favor English-language development for LEP students, rather than second-language development for English monolingual students.

• Students in cooperative groups are usually assigned roles, such as facilitator, recorder, material monitor, clean-up monitor. Care should be taken to assure that roles rotate among students. Without teacher intervention, less important roles may be assigned to minority students.

In other words, cooperative learning, like all methodologies, seems to be influenced by the social and sociolinguistic environment. English is the dominant language in the United States, and even significant and consistent efforts to reinforce the importance of other languages may not be sufficient to overcome its dominance. In addition, both majority and minority students are often socialized to accept themselves and others in certain roles. Teachers need to understand those tendencies and counter them.

Second-Language Instruction

In addition to language development through content instruction, most bilingual programs set aside time for dedicated second-language development. The great majority of programs focus on serving LEP children, and the second language being developed is usually English. Increasingly, however, programs are also offering opportunities for English monolingual students to learn a new language. Language acquisition theory and methodology are generally applicable to both groups of learners.

Traditional Approaches

Approaches and methods in second-language teaching have changed rapidly in the last fifty years as our assumptions about learning in general and language learning in particular have evolved. Until World War II, languages were usually taught as they had been for centuries, using the grammar-translation approach, with an emphasis on grammatical analysis and pencil-and-paper exercises. Those of us who experienced the grammar-translation approach can probably remember many tedious hours learning conjugations and declensions, but little, if anything at all, about the living language we were studying.

World War II created a dramatic need for military personnel proficient in a great variety of languages, many of them quite exotic from the American perspective, and some of which had no writing system at all. In response to that need, and in keeping with the behaviorist model of learning that was popular at the time, the military developed what has come to be known as the audio-lingual approach to second-language instruction. The audio-lingual approach assumes that we learn language by making it a habit. The method therefore emphasizes repetitive, structured oral drills and dialogues focused on language patterns. Oral communication is the priority, and reading and writing are added for advanced students. The audio-lingual approach as implemented in military settings also included follow-up conversations and activities with native speakers of the target language. Many classroom teachers today rely on similar audio-lingual pattern drills; they do not, however, always include opportunities for the natural conversation that was likely a key factor in the success of the original approach.

Recent Second-Language Acquisition Theory

In the 1950s, the famous linguist Noam Chomsky suggested that children learn their first language not by imitation and repetition, as was previously assumed, but rather by sorting out the underlying rules and patterns in the language they hear. This idea was revolutionary in its time, but has since been accepted and expanded to include not only underlying grammar rules but social rules as well.

The process of second-language acquisition seems to involve similar processes of rule finding, although second-language learners differ from first-language learners in that they have an already-developed understanding of the world and of language. Recent theorists propose that students acquire a second language best when they are exposed to language they can understand in real communication situations.

Stephen Krashen's (1981) theory of second-language acquisition is perhaps the best known among educators today. Krashen proposes a distinction between language acquisition and language learning. Learning is formal and focuses on rules, whereas acquisition is similar to what might be called "picking up" a language. Krashen suggests that acquisition is more important for real communication, and that students acquire a second language when they are presented with comprehensible sounds or symbols—or language they can understand—in a nonthreatening environment.

The Natural Approach

The focus on the need for real communicative settings to facilitate second-language acquisition has produced a variety of innovative communicative approaches for teaching students a second language. The application of Krashen's theory in particular has produced the Natural Approach (Terrell 1981), which is especially suited for use with primary-level students.

The Natural Approach assumes that there are four stages of language acquisition and presents methods and teacher behaviors appropriate to each stage:

1. *Preproduction.* Students at the preproduction stage communicate primarily through gestures and actions. At this stage, teachers should focus on building receptive vocabulary and listening comprehension skills through:

- Movement activities
- Visual aids
- Hands-on activities
- Opportunities for nonverbal response, like pointing, head shaking, holding up signs.

Teachers should not force production by insisting on verbal responses.

2. *Early production.* Students communicate using one or two words or short phrases. At this stage, teachers should expand receptive vocabulary and motivate students to use the vocabulary they have already acquired by:

- Providing opportunities for simple responses, such as yes-no questions (Is it a doll or a ball? Who is holding the ball now?).
- Expanding on students' answers to increase receptive vocabulary (Yes, Manuel is holding the ball. Is it red or blue? Yes, it is a blue ball.).

Teachers should not insist on verbal responses or correct students' pronunciation or syntax.

3. *Speech emergence.* Students begin to speak in longer phrases or complete sentences. At this stage, teachers should continue to expand receptive vocabulary and encourage students' use of more complex language. Teachers can:

- Include games in content instruction.
- Provide opportunities to discuss preferences, feelings, opinions, and issues that will excite discussion.
- Use photographs, charts, and other visuals as the basis for problem-solving activities that encourage discussion.

As in the early stages, teachers should not force or correct verbal responses.

4. *Intermediate production.* Students can produce connected discourse and engage in conversation. Second-language instruction for intermediate students approaches language arts instruction for native speakers. At this stage, teachers can incorporate reading and writing activities.

When implementing the Natural Approach, consider the following:

• *Communication is more important than correctness.* For most teachers this is easier to say than to act on. They tend to want to immediately correct errors in speech and often feel that if they fail to correct pronunciation or syntax, students will never learn correct forms. If teachers simply model correct forms and encourage communication, however, students will usually acquire standard language forms in the course of meaningful interaction.

- *The goal of a second-language teacher is to develop intermediate-level speakers of the language.* It is impossible to achieve language perfection in the classroom. Students need to be sufficiently equipped to encounter the outside language world, initiate conversation, understand messages, and mediate miscommunication ("Excuse me, could you repeat that?").

- *The Natural Approach is an excellent method for developing young students' oral proficiency.* As children develop oral proficiency, they should be introduced to English language arts and reading.

Approaches for Intermediate Learners

There are several approaches to second-language development that are useful for students who have gained intermediate proficiency in English but still need help in content areas where language may present difficulties apart from the subject matter. Sheltered English and the Cognitive Academic Language Learning Approach are discussed below. These approaches should not be considered replacements for bilingual programming using primary-language instruction for LEP students.

Sheltered English

In the Sheltered English approach, teachers modify and mediate instruction so as to make content comprehensible to students who are learning in a second language. Sheltered English teachers modify their language to facilitate understanding. They slow down their speech, use repetition and synonyms, and avoid highly idiomatic usage. They also mediate instruction through visual aids and hands-on activities that enhance comprehensible input.

Sheltered English teachers do not "dumb-down" content. Sheltered English does not involve remedial content.

A professional educator, when introduced to the concepts of Sheltered English, commented, "Isn't this simply good, sensitive instruction?" Clearly, the use of visual aids, hands-on activities, and carefully organized presentations are hallmarks of good instruction. Such attempts to create a context for instruction and enhance meaning are especially useful for second-language learners who need comprehensible input to expand their second-language skills and to understand subject concepts.

Cognitive Academic Language Learning Approach (CALLA)

Designed for students in grades 4 through 12, CALLA is a program designed for students who are orally proficient in English but need to develop their cognitive academic language skills. CALLA addresses three components:

• *Content instruction.* Teachers create a context for instruction, as in Sheltered English, and support it through the use of demonstrations, visual aides, and hands-on experiences.

• *Academic language skills.* Teachers help students develop language skills in the context of actual academic assignments in the content areas.

• *Learning strategies.* CALLA focuses on three kinds of learning strategies:

- Metacognitive strategies—for example, organizing, monitoring, and evaluating one's own learning.
- Cognitive strategies—for example, strategies for interacting with new material, such as note taking, repetition, making visual associations.
- Social and affective strategies—for example, ways to involve other people, like the teacher or peers, in the learning process (O'Malley and Chamot 1990).

CALLA, too, incorporates many aspects of an instructional program that might be useful to any learner. CALLA is especially helpful to students as they make the transition from learning in their primary language to learning in their new one.

Literacy in Bilingual Programs

There are two questions that come up in any discussion of bilingual programs and reading instruction: Which language should be used to teach children to read? If children learn to read in the primary language, when should the transition to reading in English occur?

Theoretically, learning to read in the primary language is easier. Once a student can read a language—any language—literacy in another·is easy to develop. We don't learn to read each time we learn a new language; many basic literacy skills transfer. So in general, bilingual programs assume that preliterate students should learn to read first in their primary language.

Note, however, that the nature of a learner's first language should be taken into account when considering literacy. Chinese, for example, does not use an alphabet with sound and symbol correspondence; each Chinese character represents a word rather than a sound. For Chinese-speaking students who are preliterate, reading in English as soon as possible may be the most sensible course, since mastery of the thousands of characters necessary for literacy in Chinese before beginning English reading would be impractical

In general, however, students in bilingual programs develop first-language literacy skills while they are developing second-language oral proficiency. Remember, though, that second-language learners do not need to fully master their new language orally before they can begin to read and write it. In fact, experience has shown that many adult learners master second-language reading and writing without ever developing much oral proficiency—for example, in cases where they need to be able to consult a particular literature for professional purposes.

With young learners, developing basic literacy skills in the language over which they have the best control is the most sensible course. As their first-language literacy skills and second-language oral proficiency grow, second-language reading and writing should be incorporated into their instructional program.

Read More About . . .

• Classroom grouping in *A Management Handbook for Bilingual Instruction*, (San Jose Calif.: San Jose Unified School District Bilingual Office, 1986).

• Cooperative learning in "Cooperative Learning and Sociocultural Factors in Schooling," by Spencer Kagan, in *Beyond Language: Social and Cultural Factors in Schooling Language Minority*

Students, edited by the California State Department of Education Office of Bilingual Bicultural Education (Los Angeles: CSU-LA Evaluation, Dissemination, and Assessment Center, 1986).

• Language testing and teaching in general in *Principles of Language Learning and Teaching,* 2nd ed., by H. Douglas Brown (Englewood Cliffs: Prentice-Hall, 1987).

• Second-language acquisition theory and classroom applications in *Making It Happen: Interaction in the Second Language Classroom from Theory to Practice,* by Patricia A. Richard-Amato (New York: Longman, 1988).

• Stephen Krashen's theory of second-language acquisition and its application in the Natural Approach in *The Natural Approach: Language Acquisition in the Classroom,* by Stephen Krashen and Tracy D. Terrell (San Francisco: Alemany Press, 1983).

• Theoretical perspectives on biliteracy in *Reading in the Bilingual Classroom: Literacy and Biliteracy,* by Kenneth Goodman, Yetta Goodman, and Barbara Flores (Rosslyn, Va.: National Clearinghouse for Bilingual Education, 1979).

• CALLA in *Learning Strategies in Second Language Acquisition,* by J. Michael O'Malley and Anna Uhl Chamot (Cambridge, Mass.: Cambridge University Press, 1990).

• Sheltered English in the *Sheltered English Teaching Handbook,* by Linda Northcutt and Daniel Watson (1986). (Available from Northcutt, Watson, Gonzales, P.O. Box 1429, Carlsbad, CA 92008.)

5

Bilingual Teachers and Aides

Who Is a Bilingual Teacher?

F ew people would suggest that all English speakers or even all English-speaking teachers have the ability to teach English. All too often, however, lay people and even some professionals assume that a teacher who speaks two languages is a bilingual teacher. Although language proficiency is clearly an important component of bilingual teaching ability, simply speaking two languages is not enough.

In 1974, a conference of experts convened by the Center for Applied Linguistics (CAL) developed a list of qualifications for bilingual teachers:

1. A thorough knowledge of the philosophy and theory concerning bilingual bicultural education and its application.

2. A genuine and sincere interest in the education of children regardless of their linguistic and cultural background, and personal qualities which contribute to success as a classroom teacher.

3. A thorough knowledge of and proficiency in the child's home language and the ability to teach content through it, an understanding of the nature of the language the child brings . . . and the ability to utilize it as a positive tool in . . . teaching.

4. Cultural awareness and sensitivity and a thorough knowledge of the cultures reflected in the two languages involved.

5. The proper professional and academic preparation obtained from a well designed teacher preparation program in bilingual-bicultural education (Center for Applied Linguistics 1974, p. 2).

Teacher competencies that support these qualities must include awareness, skills, and knowledge related to language, culture, pedagogy, and community relations.

What About Language?

State education agencies that offer bilingual certification usually test teachers for second-language ability. Although the measures vary from place to place, the common expectation is that bilingual teachers will be able to use English and the target language for all social and professional purposes, including listening, speaking, reading, and writing. Ideally a bilingual teacher is a balanced bilingual, a person who can understand, speak, read, and write two languages with equal proficiency, at the level of an educated speaker of either language.

Language proficiency for teachers, as for others, must be viewed in the context of the situations they encounter. Bilingual teachers, like all teachers, deliver instruction. To do so, they should be competent in standard varieties of both English and the target language of their classrooms, and they should be capable of delivering instruction in required skill and content areas in both languages. Teachers do more than teach, however. To put it another way, teaching involves more than delivery of instruction.

Consider the following situation: School has been in session for almost a month when Rocio comes to kindergarten. Newly arrived from Mexico, she speaks no English and is overwhelmed and bewildered by her new circumstances. Rocio cries for most of her first day at school, and her mother, worried about leaving her, sits in the back of the room.

On the following day, the teacher tactfully asks Rocio's mother to leave. It takes Rocio about twenty minutes to calm down and she remains tearful all day, requiring frequent attention and comfort.

This continues for three days, until Rocio begins to feel comfortable in her new environment.

This situation is familiar to anyone who has taught kindergarten. It is presented here to illustrate that teachers often need to communicate with parents and children in emotional or difficult situations; this requires a situationally appropriate command of language quite different from the language skills necessary for instructional purposes.

CAL guidelines point out that teachers must have "adequate control of pronunciation, vocabulary, and regional, stylistic, and nonverbal variants appropriate to the communication context" (Center for Applied Linguistics 1974, pp. 2–3). That is to say, bilingual teachers must be able to deliver instruction in a standard variety of both classroom languages. Also, they must be able to communicate with parents and students in noninstructional contexts.

The importance of the use of children's primary language in noninstructional contexts is illustrated by teachers' comments in a study done in southern California. A teacher in that study remarked: "The minute he knew I spoke Spanish he felt more comfortable in my class." "The mother showed confidence with me because I can speak the language" (Rodriguez 1980, p. 383).

Linguistic Theory

To respond effectively to students' varying stages of bilingual language development, teachers need knowledge of linguistics, psycholinguistics, and sociolinguistics. Consider this situation: The teacher holds up colored blocks and elicits Spanish color names as preparation for a math activity that involves making patterns. When he holds up the yellow block, the children chorus, "Amarillo." When he holds up the orange block, they all respond, "Jello." At that moment the teacher has to make linguistic judgments. Are these children code switching? Is this "error" appropriate to their level of language development? Or are they simply confused? The teacher stops for a moment and reviews "amarillo," "anaranjado," "yellow," and "orange."

Responding effectively to children who are developing in two languages requires an understanding of the nature of language. In addition, teachers must be knowledgeable about the processes of first- and second-language development, as well as the nature of bilingualism and the process of becoming bilingual.

Bilingual teachers must value the language that their students bring to the classroom. Language prestige and language use and learning in turn are affected by political and social contexts. On a broad scale, teachers need to understand the manifestations and implications of formal and informal language policy. On a day-to-day basis, teachers must be aware of the roles of regional and social dialects and the dynamics of language attitudes and bias.

Teachers also must possess the skills necessary to present academic content to second-language learners and the strategies necessary to help those students develop their second language. Finally, bilingual teachers must be able to assess language proficiency—both formally and informally.

Beyond Language

Tests of teacher competency in the area of culture are often multiple-choice measures containing items related to names, dates, habits, and significant accomplishments of a target group. Such lists and recipes, however, fail to respond to the real needs of children in classrooms. Consider the following incident: A Mexican American migrant farm-work student is slightly injured during recess, and the teacher in charge takes her to the nurse. Several of her brothers and sisters crowd around and attempt to accompany her to the nurse's office. The office is small, and the nurse suggests that the children return to the school yard.

Sensing the children's reluctance to leave, the teacher indicates that it would be better if they all stayed. The child's small scrape is quickly cleaned and bandaged as her siblings look on, and all the children return happily to play. The teacher understands that the children feel a strong sense of responsibility for their brothers and sisters, and that leaving their sister alone would make them uneasy. Small scrapes are a day-to-day reality on any playground, and this incident illustrates that teachers encounter cultural values at work in every facet of school life.

Teacher trainers generally agree that every teacher must develop specialized awareness, skills, and knowledge to work in culturally diverse settings. They agree less about what constitutes the culture knowledge base that teachers need to have. This is complicated by the fact that even linguistically homogeneous classrooms may be culturally diverse. For example, Spanish speakers come to California from many different parts of the United States, Mexico, and Latin America. Their cultural backgrounds are very different.

No individual teacher can know everything there is to know about all the cultures in any classroom, or even about any single culture, including her own. And as the above anecdote illustrates, bilingual teachers must respond to the values and belief systems of students in their classrooms—that is, to "implicit" rather than "explicit" characteristics of culture (Arvizu, Snyder, and Espinosa 1980).

Working in a culturally diverse setting requires an understanding of the nature of culture, with an emphasis on values and belief systems. Skills in observing and analyzing cultures and an appreciation for diversity are essential to developing an understanding of culture in general and of specific cultures represented in a classroom. Finally, children in school experience the interaction of two cultures, their own and the culture of the school. Teachers need to develop the ability to avoid the potential pitfalls and to promote the positive outcomes of the intersection of home and school cultures.

Sociocultural Issues

Teaching and learning take place in a social and cultural context. Consider this situation: District policy has structured bilingual classrooms so that no more than half the children are LEP. The instructional rationale for this format is that fluent English speakers will provide models for LEP students. Several fluent English-speaking students, however, have begun to tease the LEP students, particularly the newly arrived immigrants. The teasing is not well intentioned and runs the gamut from remarks about personal appearance to exclusion from schoolyard games. Immigrant LEP students, already overwhelmed by school, are becoming more withdrawn with each passing day. The teacher begins to implement a program that stresses positive interpersonal relations, in the hope of improving classroom climate.

The cultural diversity of the United States presents a unique set of circumstances that must be considered in a discussion of sociocultural competencies. Some Americans are newly arrived; others can trace their ancestry back centuries. Except for the descendants of the indigenous peoples of the Americas, all Americans have roots elsewhere.

The United States has been compared on the one hand to a melting pot, and on the other, to a salad bowl. The melting pot metaphor suggests that all cultures contribute ingredients to produce an amalgamated American. Salad-bowl ideology envisions each culture contributing its flavor and individuality to produce an appetizing mix. In either picture, the unique history and composition of U.S. society produce contact among cultures, which may in turn produce conflict among cultures.

Bilingual teachers need to be able to understand the dynamics of assimilation, enculturation, and acculturation. They must also understand the nature of culture conflict and be able to cultivate a positive cross-cultural classroom environment. This requires an understanding and appreciation of the history and contributions of minority cultures in the United States, and the ability to incorporate them into materials and activities.

Pedagogy

Very few modern classrooms reflect the outdated stereotypical model of children sitting quietly in rows while a teacher stands at the front of the room talking to them. Increasingly, the classroom is a place for group work, hands-on explorations, and high levels of student participation. The classroom described below is a typical contemporary classroom that uses bilingual instruction to meet the needs of LEP learners and to develop second-language skills for monolingual English-speaking students.

The kindergarten class is half LEP learners and half English monolingual students. About half the children in both language groups are ready to begin reading the preprimer. The other half are still working on prereading skills. Since half the students are working in Spanish and the other half in English, there are four reading groups.

Working with an aide, the teacher rotates the children through four centers. In the first center she provides direct instruction. In the second center her aide monitors guided practice and follow-up activities. The third center involves a hands-on readiness activity, and the fourth has listening stations with taped interactive second-language lessons and activity sheets. This organization is illustrated in Figure 5.1.

FIGURE 5.1
Bilingual Kindergarten:
Rotation During Reading and Language Arts

Personnel:	Teacher (Direct Instruction)	Aide (Follow-up)	Independent/ Parent Volunteer (Readiness/Skill Reinforcement)	Listening Station
Curriculum:	L1 Reading	L1 Reading	L1 Reading	L2 Development
Period I:	LE Beginners	LS Beginners	LE Advanced	LS Advanced
Period II:	LS Advanced	LE Beginners	LS Beginners	LE Advanced
Period III:	LE Advanced	LS Advanced	LE Beginners	LS Beginners
Period IV:	LS Beginners	LE Advanced	LS Advanced	LE Beginners

L1 = First Language
L2 = Second Language
LE = English speakers
LS = Spanish speakers

Each group spends fifteen minutes at a station, and children rotate through all the stations during the reading period. On Tuesdays and Thursdays, a parent volunteer helps supervise the hands-on activity. This is helpful because some children have difficulty staying on task in unsupervised settings.

Every teacher must be a skilled manager. In a bilingual setting, basic preparation tasks are doubled to meet the needs of children in varying stages of second-language development. Implementing dual-language instruction can be made easier with the help of a paraprofessional or other aide. As experienced teachers know, having additional personnel in the classroom means added benefits for the students (though added management tasks for the teacher in charge).

To manage a bilingual classroom, teachers must be able to assess language proficiency and academic achievement and plan and organize instruction that is appropriate to all students' abilities. They must also plan and organize instruction that fosters second-language development. Often, bilingual teachers are called on to develop materials or critically review and modify existing materials to meet the needs of bilingual learners. Finally, managing a bilingual learning environment requires teachers to plan for and supervise additional personnel and community volunteers.

Community Relations

C onsider the following situation. In a district that has many recently arrived Vietnamese-speaking students, bilingual teachers have customarily been assisted by teacher aides during reading time. At a school board meeting, two newly elected board members question the need for extra staffing in bilingual classrooms. At the following meeting, a bilingual resource teacher makes a presentation on the bilingual program.

In the course of the discussion, it becomes clear that one of the board members is disturbed by the idea of any primary-language instruction at all. "Why should we spend public money," he asks, "to teach children in Vietnamese? Shouldn't they learn English as quickly as possible?" In the short time available, the teacher develops, in layman's terms, a rationale for primary-language instruction. Although the official is still somewhat skeptical, the presentation seems to have moderated his position.

Bilingual teachers are often called on to make presentations to professional and lay groups. Because bilingual instruction is generally controversial and misunderstood, bilingual teachers should be able to articulate, in both professional and lay terms, theories and methods of bilingual instruction.

Bilingual teachers are also often called on to be child advocates, bringing the needs of a child whose parents may not speak English or understand procedures to the attention of the educational or social service systems. Acting as a liaison between community, schools, and language-minority families requires that bilingual teachers be familiar with the community served by the school. Bilingual teachers are often asked to talk with language-minority parents and clarify how the parents and the school can work together.

The Role of Paraprofessionals

In the classroom, aides have traditionally been responsible for clerical tasks, such as record keeping, filing, copying, and housekeeping tasks, including assembling materials for instruction, replenishing materials, and supervising students' clean-up. Outside the classroom, aides have been responsible for noninstructional tasks, such as cafeteria and yard duty, loading and unloading school buses, accompanying children to the nurse's office, and assisting on field trips.

Increasingly, however, paraprofessionals are involved in instructional supervision and support. For example, paraprofessionals often help children locate resources for projects or group work. They may also provide make-up lessons for children who have been absent. In addition, they may supervise guided practice and reinforcement activities that follow direct instruction by the teacher.

According to the California State Department of Education (1984), the complex environment of a bilingual classroom requires teachers to team with their aides. Bilingual paraprofessionals, often members of the ethnic community of the LEP learners, can assist in significant ways. In addition to providing instructional support, a bilingual aide in a team relationship with a teacher can:

• Help students develop language skills and learn more about the culture of their community.

• Enhance home/school communication.

• Provide a community role model (California State Department of Education 1984, p. 20).

Expanding the traditional role of the paraprofessional to roles involving instruction and even leadership requires that attention be given to appropriate training programs for teacher aides. Paraprofessionals should be trained in basic methodologies and general classroom management. To assist in meeting the needs of LEP students, training should include discussion of theories of first-language development and second-language acquisition. Paraprofessionals need to understand the cultural and historical perspectives of LEP students. Training should also include the development of language and literacy skills in the non-English language and, if necessary, the development of English language skills.

Finally, paraprofessionals and teachers need to be trained to work together. Inservices for bilingual teachers and aides should include a component that will allow them to build a team and learn strategies for cooperation in the classroom.

Read More About . . .

• Bilingual teacher competencies in "Competencies for Bilingual Multicultural Teachers," by S. Ana Garza and Carol P. Barnes, in *The Journal of Educational Issues of Language Minority Students* 5 (Fall 1989): 1–25.

• The role of paraprofessionals in *Bilingual-Crosscultural Teacher Aides: A Resource Guide* (Sacramento: California State Department of Education, 1984).

6

The Rights of Limited-English-Proficient Students

How Many LEP Students Are There?

A recent *Newsweek* article comments, "In small towns and big cities, children with names like Oswaldo, Sunong, Boris or Ngam are swelling the rolls in U.S. public schools, sitting side by side with Dick and Jane" (February 11, 1991, p. 56). The article goes on to report that approximately 9 million people immigrated to the United States in the 1980s, a greater number than reached our shores in the first ten years of the century.

LEP students are no longer isolated cases in otherwise English-speaking schools. There are between 3.5 and 5.3 million LEP children between the ages of five and thirteen in the United States (Ambert 1988). Again, from *Newsweek* (1991): "In seven states including Colorado, New Mexico, New York and Texas, 25 percent or more of the students are not native-English speakers. All but a handful of states have at least 1,000 foreign born youngsters."

The Council of Chief State School Officers (1990) reports that New Jersey has an LEP student population of 36,000 students, or 9 percent of the total public school population. Massachusetts has 80,000 LEP students or about 10 percent of its total enrollment.

Texas has an LEP population of more than 300,000 students (the second-largest LEP enrollment of any state). California's 1990 DATA/BICAL, its annual census of LEP students reports 861,531 LEP students in grades K–12, or about 15 percent of its public school enrollment. California has the largest LEP enrollment of any state, both in number and percentage.

California is a bellwether for demographic change, and its public schools currently serve students speaking any one of about 100 languages. In some schools, as many as twenty-two languages may be represented on any given day. Nationwide, about 150 languages are represented in the public schools.

As the number of LEP students grows and language diversity increases, districts around the country have tried to implement effective academic approaches to meet the needs of students who lack the English language skills necessary to succeed in English-only classrooms. Often, attempts to provide services are surrounded by controversy, prompting us to ask: What services, if any, are school districts required to provide for LEP students?

Federal Policy and Bilingual Education

There are no federal laws that mandate bilingual education. There is, however, legislation that provides funding and support for services to limited-English-proficient students. In addition, federal court decisions, focused primarily on civil rights for non-English speakers, support an entitlement to services that offer equal educational opportunity to LEP students.

Title VII: The Bilingual Education Act

Signed into law in 1968, Title VII of the Elementary and Secondary Education Act (ESEA), known as the Bilingual Education Act, provides funds for direct services to students, teacher training, and support services such as technical assistance and dissemination of information. Since 1968 there have been reauthorizations of the Act with amendments in 1974, 1978, 1984, and 1988. The next reauthorization is scheduled for 1993. Title VII funds have increased with each reauthorization and current funding is approximately

$186 million. Figure 6.1 on pages 59–61 lists current projects funded by Title VII. Note, however, that funding fails to keep pace with the growing need. Only 10 percent of programs aimed at LEP students are currently funded by Title VII. The remaining 90 percent are funded by local and state education agencies (*Forum*, January 1991, p. 2).

Title VII funds are discretionary; that is, they are not automatically available to every student who is assessed as LEP. Funds are awarded to state and local educational agencies, universities, and other educational institutions through a competitive proposal writing process.

Although Title VII does not mandate bilingual education, the Act effectively establishes policy at the national level through its acknowledgement of the needs of LEP students. Recent modifications of the legislation accommodate the diversity of languages and needs in the schools and give local educational agencies discretion in implementing programs. It is clear from Title VII, however, that native-language instruction is an acceptable and even desirable means of assisting LEP students while they learn English. Attempts by legislators and bureaucrats to alter or erode that intention have repeatedly failed.

Lau v. Nichols (1974)

We cannot discuss the legal bases for bilingual education without mentioning the landmark United States Supreme Court decision in *Lau v. Nichols*. It should be noted at the outset, however, that although *Lau* is important from a historical perspective, its practical significance has diminished.

In 1974 a group of Chinese students sued the San Francisco Unified School District. In their suit the plaintiffs claimed that they were denied access to a meaningful education because they could not understand the education they received. They claimed the school violated Title VI of the Civil Rights Act of 1964, which prohibits discrimination on the basis of race, color, or national origin.

The Court found for the plaintiffs, but did not specify a remedy for their complaint. Instead, the Court noted that several solutions were possible, including native-language instruction and ESL classes. As Piatt has noted (1990), *Lau* did not establish a constitutional right to bilingual education or even a requirement that districts provide primary-language content instruction.

Lau was, however, a catalyst for public policy. In the wake of the *Lau* decision, for example, New York City entered into a consent decree in the *Aspira* case and significantly expanded services to LEP students in New York City. The Department of Health, Education, and Welfare also promulgated regulations regarding the identification and assessment of LEP students and the delivery of services to them. Although the regulations were never formally adopted, they were used as a de facto guide to *Lau* compliance by school districts and consequently had a far-reaching effect on programming for LEP students across the country. In addition, after *Lau*, several states enacted legislation mandating services for LEP students.

The Equal Educational Opportunities Act (1974)

Since *Lau*, various court decisions have reshaped judicial interpretation of Title VI of the Civil Rights Act (Heubert 1988, Crawford 1989) and have mitigated the power of *Lau* as a protection for LEP student rights. The strongest federal protection for the educational rights of LEP students is currently the Equal Educational Opportunities Act (EEOA). Section 1703(f) of the Act states:

> No State shall deny equal educational opportunity to an individual on account of his or her race, color, sex, or national origin by . . . (f) the failure by an educational agency to take appropriate steps to overcome language barriers that impede equal participation by its students in its instructional programs.

The focus of the EEOA was school busing, and there is no elaboration in the law on the rights of LEP students. The meaning of Section 1703(f) and its impact on programming for LEP students has been derived, therefore, from judicial interpretation, which has focused on the phrase "appropriate action." What must school districts do to protect the rights afforded to LEP students by the EEOA? The standard for complying with the legislation has evolved from several federal court cases: *Castañeda v. Pickard*, 1981; *Idaho Migrant Council v. Board of Education*, 1981; *Keyes v. School District No. 1*, 1983; and *Gomez v. Illinois State Board of Education*, 1987. The basic requirement that derives from these cases is that LEP students must receive equal access to the curriculum. "Appropriate action" as interpreted by federal courts includes:

• A program based on sound educational theory.
• The allocation of trained personnel and the material resources necessary to implement the program.
• An evaluation and feedback process.

Equal access as defined by the courts does not require bilingual programs. Equal access does, however, prohibit districts from placing LEP students in classrooms where they cannot understand the language being spoken. A careful reading of federal case law would suggest that districts should provide an affirmative program that:

• Addresses the development of English language skills for LEP students, and
• Assures that LEP students do not learn less because of their lack of knowledge of English.

State Law

I n the 1970s following *Lau*, many states passed legislation mandating services to LEP students. In the 1980s, however, as federal support for bilingual education became more uncertain, several states, including California and Colorado, eliminated their mandates for bilingual education.

In states that have bilingual education laws, the requirements for services to LEP students are fairly straightforward. State laws provide for the identification and assessment of LEP students, describe program options to serve them, and specify requirements for staffing. Also, state laws usually set forth requirements for parent involvement. In states where broad-scale bilingual programs are mandated, such as Arizona, Illinois, Indiana, Massachusetts, Rhode Island, and Texas, the emphasis is generally on transitional programming, although other forms of programs are allowed. Twenty-two states now have bilingual education statutes (Piatt 1990).

A State Without a Mandate: California

Not all states with large populations of LEP students mandate bilingual programs. California is the prime example. From 1980 to 1987 the Chacon-Moscone Bilingual-Bicultural Education Act mandated bilingual programs in California. Under that law, districts were required to establish bilingual classrooms staffed by certified bilingual teachers if a school had ten or more LEP students at the same grade level, speaking the same primary language. Individualized services were required in cases where classrooms were not warranted by numbers, and at the secondary level. Provisions of the law also addressed parent involvement.

California's bilingual education mandate lapsed in 1987 when the governor vetoed its reauthorization. As a result of a quirk in California state law, however, districts are still required to carry out the original purposes of the law. The original purposes of the bilingual education law are vaguely stated, and in the absence of a clear mandate, services vary extensively from district to district. Many districts with large populations of LEP students maintain programs comparable to those previously required. Others are experimenting with various forms of ESL instruction and sheltered methodologies.

One such program was challenged in federal court in *Teresa P. v. Berkeley Unified School District* in 1989. In that case, advocates for services for LEP students tried to clarify the meaning of "appropriate action" as it appears in the EEOA, hoping to strengthen the standards set forth in other federal cases and broaden their application with a comparable decision in California. Unfortunately, the court's decision in *Teresa P.* was vague and narrow, and it failed to set a direction for California's public schools.

The Florida Consent Decree

Florida, another state with a large population of LEP students, had no statewide standards for serving them until 1990. Recently, as a result of a lawsuit by a coalition of agencies representing the interests of LEP students, Florida entered into a consent decree that outlines a plan for serving LEP students. Under the provisions of the plan, LEP students will be identified and assessed, programming aimed at providing access to the curriculum will be implemented, teachers will be trained in ESL and bilingual methodologies, principals and administrators will be trained in the provisions of the consent decree, and outcome measures will be developed. In other words, Florida has consented to establish services that meet the criteria developed in the federal courts to define "appropriate action."

Read More About . . .

• The legal foundations of bilingual education. Laws change constantly and vary from state to state. Current information is available from state educational agencies. To keep practitioners up-to-date, the National Clearinghouse for Bilingual Education publishes *Forum*, a monthly newsletter that contains information on a variety of pertinent subjects, including legislation, programs, resources, conferences, and professional organizations. *Forum* is available by calling 1-800-321-NCBE.

FIGURE 6.1
1990 Title VII Funding

PROGRAM	PURPOSE	RECIPIENT	NO. OF PROGRAMS CURRENTLY FUNDED	FUNDING (in millions of dollars)
Transitional Bilingual Education Programs	To help elementary and secondary LEP students acquire English skills while meeting academic goals with primary-language instruction when necessary.	LEAs; IHEs in collaboration with LEAs	Approx. 518 (awards in progress)	80.0
Developmental Bilingual Education Programs	To provide bilingual instruction to LEP and English monolingual students.	LEAs; IHEs in collaboration with LEAs	17	3.0
Special Alternative Education Programs	To provide services to LEP students that do not involve primary-language instruction.	LEAs; IHEs, including 2-year colleges, in collaboration with LEAs	171	17.9
Family English Literacy Programs	To provide English language development programs for LEP adults and out-of-school youth.	LEAs, IHEs, private nonprofit organizations	37	4.9
Special Populations Programs	To assist preschool, special education, and gifted and talented programs serving LEP students.	LEAs, IHEs, private nonprofit organizations	48	7.4

LEA = Local education agency   SEA = State Education agency   IHE = Institution of higher education

Source: OBEMLA 1990

(Continued)

FIGURE 6.1 *(Continued)*
1990 Title VII Funding

PROGRAM	PURPOSE	RECIPIENT	NO. OF PROGRAMS CURRENTLY FUNDED	FUNDING (in millions of dollars)
Academic Excellence Programs	To support the development of training materials and to reach out to other programs and institutions.	LEAs, IHEs, private nonprofit organizations	12	2.1
Educational Personnel Training Programs	To support training of educational personnel.	Students in IHEs at undergraduate and master's levels	114	16.8
Bilingual Education Fellowship Programs	To support advanced training in bilingual education in areas such as teacher training, program evaluation, administration, and research.	IHEs	30	2.0
Training, Development, and Improvement Programs	To support innovation and improvement in graduate education, and faculty recruitment in bilingual education.	IHEs	11	1.0
Short-Term Training Programs	To support activities to improve skills of educational personnel and parents.	LEAs, SEAs IHEs, private profit and nonprofit organizations	18	1.7

Program	Purpose	Recipients	Number	Amount (millions)
State Education Agency Programs	To assist SEAs in collection, analysis, and reporting of data on LEP students and services. Also, to provide support services for program implementation.	SEAs	55	5.9
Emergency Immigrant Education Programs	To support supplemental educational services to eligible immigrant children.	SEAs	33	30.1
Evaluation Assistance Centers (EACs)*	To provide technical assistance regarding student assessment and program evaluation to SEAs and LEAs with Title VII programs.	IHEs	2	1.1
Multifunctional Resource Centers (MRCs)**	To provide technical assistance and training to educational personnel and parents; to gather and disseminate information on designated areas of bilingual education to other MRCs.	IHEs, private profit and nonprofit organizations	16	9.4
National Clearinghouse for Bilingual Education (NCBE)	To collect, analyze, and disseminate information about bilingual education. Services include a reference and referral service and computerized data base. NCBE publishes a bimonthly newsletter and occasional papers.	IHEs, private profit and nonprofit organizations	1	2.7

* = Currently funded EACs are listed in Appendix A.   ** = Currently funded MRCs are listed in Appendix B.

7

Questions People Often Ask About Bilingual Education

Bilingual Education—A Hot Topic

Bilingual education seems to excite a lot of controversy. People have powerful emotional responses to language and culture and strong opinions about public education, and the introduction of bilingual education can produce a volatile mixture. This book has attempted to present a cool, even-handed look at the issues involved in bilingual education. What follows are some of the most commonly asked questions about bilingual education. Some of the answers may recapitulate material presented earlier in the book, but they are included for review and emphasis. Also included are suggestions for further reading for readers who want to pursue issues in depth.

If I don't speak a language other than English, or if I have students with several different primary languages in my classroom, are there any strategies I can use to assist them?

To assist limited-English-proficient learners in any classroom, teachers should:

• *Create a predictable classroom environment.* Establishing routines, marking transitions between activities, and using clear signals, all assist an LEP learner in understanding expectations. Consistent routines also allow LEP learners to make connections between activities and the language that accompanies them.

• *Build academic language skills.* Teachers usually identify new and important vocabulary for all students. LEP learners may need help with process vocabulary. Words like "list," "compare," "describe," or "explain" may be unfamiliar and should be reviewed for students working in a second language.

• *Provide context for activities.* Use visuals and hands-on activities whenever possible to help provide comprehensible language input.

• *Use questions effectively.* Be sure to leave enough time for a response, because second-language learners may need more time than native speakers to answer a question. Listen for meaning in the answer rather than correctness of speech, and acknowledge correct content. Repeat students' answers and paraphrase them if necessary to model correct language forms. Provide opportunities for nonverbal responses to questions: For example, ask students to indicate a response on a map, a chart, or a graph.

• *Facilitate understanding.* Check your comprehension of what a student says. If necessary, repeat and rephrase questions and answers. Listen for communication, not correctness. Constant correction stifles communication. When communication is emphasized, students will generate language and receive language input, which will assist in their language development.

Language is an important component of instruction and modifying language can ease the experience of a student working in a new language. Other important considerations come into play, however, in classrooms characterized by diversity. Educators will enjoy reading *Embracing Diversity: Teachers' Voices From California's Classrooms*, by Laurie Olsen and Nina Mullen (San Francisco: California Tomorrow, 1990). Through profiles of teachers and analysis of their methods, *Embracing Diversity* describes mainstream teachers who work effectively with diverse student groups.

What is the best age to learn a second language?

People generally assume that children learn a second language better and faster than adults do. Although the idea of a "critical period" prior to puberty has some support among psycholinguists, current thinking indicates that this is not the case. Children do seem to learn a second language with a nativelike accent that most adult second-language learners are unlikely to attain. This may be due in part to the neurological maturation process of brain lateralization, which seems to limit the plasticity of the brain. Another possible explanation is that children have better psychomotor skills than adults, and that those skills help them master the phonological system of a language.

In any event, mastery of the phonological system is not necessary for language proficiency. H. Douglas Brown, whose book *Principles of Language Learning and Teaching* is a classic in the field, makes the following observation:

> Pronunciation of a language is not by any means the sole criterion for acquisition, nor is it really the most important one. We all know people who have less than perfect pronunciation but who also have magnificent and fluent control of a second language, control that can even exceed that of many native speakers. I like to call this the 'Henry Kissinger' effect in honor of the former U.S. secretary of State whose German accent was so noticeable yet who was clearly more eloquent than the large majority of native speakers of American English (Brown 1987, pp. 46–47).

Although age may have some bearing on the ability to acquire a second language, other factors come into play as well. For example, personality may play a role in second-language learning. Extroverted, confident people are more likely to attempt communication in a new language and thereby generate the language input that seems to facilitate learning. Motivation is also a factor. An individual may be motivated, for example, to learn a new language if it will result in career advancement. Cultural factors, attitudes, and biases may affect a person's motivation to learn a language. In many places in the world, bilingualism is the norm, and people learn more than one language without much fanfare—indeed, without schooling!

Factors affecting second-language acquisition are discussed in detail in Brown's book. Readers may also want to consult *Mirror of Language: The Debate on Bilingualism*, by Kenji Hakuta (New York: Basic Books, 1986).

When should LEP students be removed from bilingual classrooms?

In keeping with current thinking on the need for students to develop cognitive academic language proficiency, or empowering language, in English, students should ideally receive five to seven years of primary-language support before they are expected to function in English-only classrooms.

In practice, early-exit transitional programs are common. Students are generally moved to English-only classrooms when they have exceeded predetermined cut-off scores on standardized achievement tests in English. Cut-off scores are generally determined by state or local policy and are often well below the 50th percentile. Such policies have the unfortunate effect of moving students to English-only classrooms before they are academically ready.

Critics of bilingual education suggest that students who have had primary-language support do not succeed in English-only classrooms. Advocates of bilingual education suggest that students need more primary-language support than they usually get. The results of a study commissioned by the United States Department of Education indicate that primary-language support does help students achieve, but the benefits for early-exit students are short-lived; on the other hand, LEP students who receive primary-language support through the 6th grade are more successful academically than other at-risk students (U.S. Department of Education 1991).

Educators interested in reviewing successful program models may want to read *On Course: Bilingual Education's Success in California*, by Stephen Krashen and Douglas Biber (Sacramento: California Association for Bilingual Education, 1988). *On Course* provides detailed data on the academic outcomes of seven effective bilingual programs in California.

We speak two languages at home. How can we raise a bilingual child?

Studies of the early acquisition of more than one language are not numerous. They are necessarily case studies, often done by psycholinguists who have children. Such research may be somewhat unsystematic, and may be biased. It is clear, however, that around the world many children are raised "bilingual as a first language."

Grosjean, in his book *Life With Two Languages* (1982), reports four strategies that have been commonly tried by parents who want to raise bilingual children:

• One person, one language, or separation of language by person.

• Minority language in the home, majority language outside, or separation of language by place.

• Language separated by time or situation, for example, one language in the morning, the other in the afternoon.

• One language initially, and a second between the ages of three and five.

"One person, one language" is probably the most common approach that parents take. Any approach, however, is subject to the effects of the child's sociolinguistic environment. A child who learns a low-status language may have difficulty maintaining that language once schooling starts. Parents who are highly motivated to maintain their home language should seek out additive bilingual programs for their children.

What are the rights of undocumented students?

In 1982, the United States Supreme Court ruled in *Plyler v. Doe*, 457 U.S. 202 (1982), that under the Equal Protection Clause of the Fourteenth Amendment public schools cannot deny children access to public education based on the children's immigration status. Specifically, schools may not:

• Bar a student from school on the basis of immigration status.

• Classify a student as a non-resident based on undocumented status.

• Inquire about a student's immigration status.

• Make inquiries of a student or parents which might expose their undocumented status.

• Require the social security numbers of all students (Carrera 1989).

Information on *Plyler* rights is detailed in *Immigrant Students: Their Legal Right of Access to the Public Schools*, by J. W. Carrera (Boston: National Coalition of Advocates for Students, 1989). NCAS also publishes *New Voices: Immigrant Students in U.S. Public Schools* (1988), which describes the challenges facing immigrant students and makes policy recommendations to schools and other government agencies.

Two other excellent sources of information on the needs of immigrant students and approaches to meeting them are: *Crossing the Schoolhouse Border*, by Laurie Olsen and Marcia Chen, (San Francisco: California Tomorrow, 1988), and *Bridges: Promising Programs for the Education of Immigrant Children*, by Laurie Olsen and Carol Dowell (San Francisco: California Tomorrow, 1989).

In keeping with the right to access established by the *Plyler* decision, immigrant children of any status who are identified as having limited English proficiency are entitled to appropriate assistance.

Should the United States have an official language policy?

All over the world, knowledge of English is considered essential. The majority of English speakers in the world have learned it as a second language for scholarship, business, and diplomacy. In the United States everyone—including immigrants, refugees, and indigenous minorities—is aware of the need to learn English. English is neither dead nor dying, as is usually the case with a language whose speakers feel the need for protective legislation. What then motivates us to consider mandating English as our official language?

U.S. English, the group spearheading the movement, is a spinoff of the efforts of the Federation for American Immigration Reform, whose agenda has been to limit immigration. Immigration has been a constant in United States history and has invariably been accompanied by nativist movements. Such reactionary movements have left us the embarrassing legacy of the Know-Nothing movement, which tried to exclude Irish Catholics from holding public office; the Chinese Exclusion Act, which halted immigration from China; and the Barred Zone Act, prohibiting Asians from obtaining citizenship—to cite just a few examples.

Our national immigration policy changed in 1965, and we now admit equal numbers of people from every country in the world, with exceptions for some people with special refugee status. The diversity of newcomers heightens their presence in our minds and excites our xenophobia, provoking us to nativist thinking, which is manifested in the English-only movement.

An enforced English-only policy would limit programs and services such as court translations, translation assistants in hospitals, and other related public services for those who require them. It would eliminate bilingual balloting, thus limiting citizens' access to the political process. It would limit the amount of time children spend in bilingual education programs, despite the research that demonstrates the benefits of primary-language instruction. An official language policy would create a two-tier system, with the doors to opportunity and services closed to those who haven't learned English.

People tend to learn the languages they need to succeed in daily life and to resist the languages imposed on them. We would do better as a society to focus our energy on providing English-as-a-second-language classes for the many adults who are on waiting lists at our night schools and community colleges. The English-only movement is authoritarian and un-American. English maintains its status in the United States without forcible imposition.

A detailed analysis of the politics of the English-only movement is available in *Bilingual Education: History, Politics, Theory and Practice*, by James Crawford (Trenton, N.J.: Crane, 1990). Two recent publications devoted to this issue are *The English-Only Question: An Official Language for Americans?*, by Dennis Baron (New Haven: Yale University Press, 1990), and *Only English? Law and Language Policy in the United States*, by Bill Piatt (Albuquerque: University of New Mexico Press, 1990).

Why is bilingual education a politically charged issue?

People who are opposed to bilingual education usually are not opposed to bilingualism per se, but feel strongly that primary-language instruction should not be made available to language-minority or LEP students. This opposition exists despite ample evidence that primary-language instruction improves the academic performance of students who have not mastered English well enough to function in English-only classrooms. There is also ample evidence that public policy support for bilingualism would be economically and politically beneficial for us as a nation. Nevertheless, opposition to bilingual education continues.

To understand the nature of this opposition, we must travel beyond pedagogical boundaries and enter the world of political considerations. One scholar (Moran 1987) has suggested that minority support and mainstream opposition stem from the recognition that publicly funded bilingual programs represent public support for minority languages, cultures, and values.

Cummins elaborated on this perspective in *Empowering Minority Students*, in which he suggests that "the fear that has engendered such a negative reaction to bilingual education is the fear of social change, of minority empowerment" (1989, pp. 109–110). Bilingual programs do, in fact, seek to empower minority populations by:

• Making the school accessible to parents in a language they understand.

• Providing an instructional curriculum that is reflective of, and responsive to, the minority groups in a particular community.

• Giving LEP students equal access to the curriculum.

Who should receive a bilingual education?

Everyone.

BIBLIOGRAPHY

Aldemir, S. R. (Fall 1989). "Bilingualism and Its Relationship to Cognitive Development." *Educational Issues of Language Minority Students* 5: 56–63.

Arvizu, S., W. A. Snyder, and P. T. Espinosa, (1980).*Demystifying the Concept of Culture: Theoretical and Conceptual Tools.* Los Angeles: CSU-LA, EDAC.

Ambert, A. N. (1988). *Bilingual Education and English as a Second Language: A Research Handbook, 1986–1987.* New York: Garland Publishing.

Aspira of New York v. Board of Education of the City of New York, Civ. No. 4002 (S.D. N.Y. consent agreement, August 29, 1974).

Baker, C. (1988). *Key Issues in Bilingualism and Bilingual Education.* Clevedon, Avon: Multilingual Matters.

Baron, D. (1990). *The English-Only Question: An Official Language for Americans?* New Haven: Yale University Press.

Bilingual Education Act of 1968, as amended, 20 U.S.C. sec. 3221 et seq.

Bilingual Education Office, Categorical Support Program Division. (1990). *Bilingual Education Handbook.* Sacramento: California State Department of Education.

Brown, H. D. (1987). *Principles of Language Learning and Teaching,* 2nd ed. Englewood Cliffs, N.J.: Prentice Hall.

California State Department of Education. (1984).*Bilingual-Crosscultural Teacher Aides: A Resource Guide.* Sacramento.

California State Department of Education. (1990).*Bilingual Education Handbook: Designing Instruction for LEP Students.* Sacramento.

Canale, M., and M. Swain. (1980). "Theoretical Bases of Communicative Approaches to Second Language Teaching and Testing." *Applied Linguistics* 1: 1–47.

Carrera, J. W. (1989). *Immigrant Students: Their Legal Right of Access to Public Schools.* Boston: National Coalition of Advocates for Students.

Castañeda v. Pickard, 648 F.2d 989 (5th Cir. 1981).

Castellanos, D. (1983). *The Best of Two Worlds: Bilingual Bicultural Education in the U. S.* Trenton: New Jersey State Department of Education.

Center for Applied Linguistics. (1974). *Guidelines for the Preparation and Certification of Teachers of Bilingual Bicultural Education.* Washington, D.C. ERIC ED# 098 809.

Chacon-Moscone Bilingual-Bicultural Education Act, Cal. Educ. Code sec. 52160.

Civil Rights Act of 1964, 42 U.S.C. sec. 2000(d).

Clark, J. L. D., and J. Lett (1988). "A Research Agenda." In *Second Language Proficiency Assessment: Current Issues*, edited by P. Lowe, Jr. and C. Stansfield. Englewood Cliffs, N.J.: Prentice-Hall.

Collier, V. P., and W. P. Thomas. (1987). "Age and Rate of Acquisition of Second Language for Academic Purposes." *TESOL Quarterly* 21, 4: 617–641.

Council of Chief State School Officers (1990). *The Challenge and the State Response: School Success for Limited English Proficient Students.* Washington, D.C.: CCSSO Resource Center on Educational Equity.

Cummins, J. (1981). "The Role of Primary Language Development in Promoting Educational Success for Language Minority Students." In *Schooling and Language Minority Students: A Theoretical Framework.* Los Angeles: EDAC, California State University, Los Angeles.

Cummins, J. (1989). *Empowering Minority Students.* Sacramento: California Association for Bilingual Education.

Cummins, J., and M. Swain. (1986). *Bilingualism in Education.* London: Longman.

Equal Educational Opportunities Act of 1974, 20 U.S.C. 1703(f).

Escamilla, K. (1980). "German-English Bilingual Schools 1870–1917: Cultural and Linguistic Survival in St. Louis." *Bilingual Journal* 52, 2: 16–20.

Forum (January 1991). "Interview with Rita Esquivel." Washington, D.C.: National Clearinghouse for Bilingual Education.

Garza, S. A., and C. P. Barnes. (1989). "Competencies for Bilingual Multicultural Teachers." *The Journal of Educational Issues of Language Minority Students* 5: 1–25.

Genesee, F. (1987). *Learning Through Two Languages: Studies of Immersion and Bilingual Education.* Cambridge, Mass.: Newbury House.

Goodman, K., Y. Goodman, and B. Flores (1979). *Reading in the Bilingual Classroom: Literacy and Biliteracy.* Rosslyn, Va.: National Clearinghouse for Bilingual Education.

Gomez v. Illinois State Board of Education, 811 F.2d 1030 (7th Cir. 1987).

Grosjean, F. (1982). *Life with Two Languages: An Introduction to Bilingualism.* Cambridge: Harvard University Press.

Hakuta, K. (1986). *Mirror of Language: The Debate on Bilingualism.* New York: Basic Books.

Harper's Index. (February 1989). *Harper's* 280, 1677:17.

Harper's Index. (November 1990). *Harper's* 281, 1686:13

Heubert, J. (1988). "Current Legal Issues in Bilingual Education." In *Bilingual Education and English as a Second Language: A Research Handbook, 1986–1987*, edited by Alba N. Ambert. New York: Garland Publishing.

Idaho Migrant Council v. Board of Education, 647 F.2d 69 (9th Circ. 1981).

Keyes v. School District No. 1, Denver, Colorado, 576 F. Supp. 1503

(D. Colo. 1983).

Kloss, H. (1977). *The American Bilingual Tradition.* Rowley, Mass.: Newbury House.

Krashen, S. (1981). "Bilingual Education and Second Language Acquisition theory." In *Schooling and Language Minority Students: A Theoretical Framework,* edited by the California State Department of Education, Office of Bilingual Bicultural Education. Los Angeles: CSU-LA Evaluation, Dissemination and Assessment Center.

Krashen, S., and D. Biber. (1988). *On Course: Bilingual Education's Success in California.* Sacramento: California Association for Bilingual Education.

Lau v. Nichols, 414 U.S. 563 (1974).

Lessow-Hurley, J. (1990). *The Foundations of Dual Language Instruction.* White Plains, N.Y.: Longman.

Miller, J. M. (October 31, 1990). "Native-Language Instruction Found to Aid L.E.P.'s." *Education Week:* 1, 23.

Moran, R. (1987). "Bilingual Education as a Status Conflict." *California Law Review* 75: 321–361.

National Coalition of Advocates for Students. (1988). *New Voices: Immigrant Students in U.S. Public Schools.* Boston: NCAS.

National Defense Education Act, 20 U.S.C. sec. 401 *et seq.,* P.L. 85-864, 72 Stat. 1580.

Newsweek (February 11, 1991). "Classrooms of Babel," pp. 56–57.

OBEMLA. (October 1990). *OBEMLA Funded Profiles.* Washington, D.C.: U.S. Department of Education, Office of Bilingual Education and Minority Languages Affairs.

Olsen, L., and M. Chen. (1988). *Crossing the Schoolhouse Border: Immigrant Students and the California Public Schools.* San Francisco: California Tomorrow.

Olsen, L., and C. Dowell. (1989). *Bridges: Promising Programs for the Education of Immigrant Children.* San Francisco: California Tomorrow.

Olsen, L., and N. A. Mullen. (1990). *Embracing Diversity: Teachers' Voices From California's Classrooms.* San Francisco: California Tomorrow.

O'Malley, J. M., and A. U. Chamot (1990). *Learning Strategies in Second Language Acquisition.* Cambridge, Mass.: Cambridge University Press.

Ovando, C. J., and V. P. Collier. (1985). *Bilingual and ESL Classrooms: Teaching in Multicultural Contexts.* New York: McGraw-Hill.

Piatt, B. (1990). *Only English? Law and Language Policy in the United States.* Albuquerque: University of New Mexico Press.

Plyler v. Doe, 457 U.S. 202 (1982).

Richard-Amato, P. A. (1988). *Making It Happen: Interaction in the Second Language Classroom, From Theory to Practice.* New York: Longman.

Rodriguez, A. M. (1980). "Empirically Defining Competencies for Effective Bilingual Teachers: A Preliminary Study." In *Ethnoperspectives in Bilingual Education Research.* Volume II, *Theory in Bilingual Education,* edited by R. V. Padilla. Ypsilanti: Department of Foreign Languages and Bilingual Studies, Eastern Michigan University.

Simon, P. (1980). *The Tongue-Tied American.* New York: Continuum.

Teresa P. v. Berkeley Unified School District, 724 F.Supp. (N.D. Cal. 1989).

Terrell, T. D. (1981). "The Natural Approach in Bilingual Education." In *Schooling and Language Minority Students: A Theoretical Framework,* edited by the California State Department of Education, Office of Bilingual Bicultural Education. Los Angeles: CSU-LA Evaluation,Dissemination and Assessment Center.

U.S. Department of Education. (February 11, 1991). *United States Department of Education News.* Washington, D.C.

Voting Rights Act of 1965, as amended, 42 U.S.C. sec. 1973, et seq.

Appendix A

Evaluation Assistance Centers Funded by Title VII (1990)

Evaluation Assistance Centers (EACs) provide technical assistance to state and local education agencies regarding methods for assessing the needs of LEP students. They also provide technical assistance for Title VII program evaluations.

EAC-East
J. Michael O'Malley, Director
Georgetown University
1916 Wilson Blvd., Suite 207
Rosslyn, VA 22209
(703) 875-0900
(800) 258-0802

EAC-West
Paul Martinez, Director
University of New Mexico
College of Education
Albuquerque, NM 87131
(505) 277-7281

Appendix B

Multifunctional Resource Centers Funded by Title VII (1990)

Multifunctional Resource Centers (MRCs) provide technical assistance to educational personnel in bilingual programs. In addition, each MRC is responsible for gathering and disseminating information to other MRCs in a designated area related to bilingual education.

Service Area 1: Connecticut, Maine, Massachusetts, New Hampshire, Rhode Island, Vermont

Adeline Becker, Director
Brown University
345 Blackstone Boulevard, Weld Bldg.
Providence, RI 02906
(401) 274-9548

Service Area 2: New York State
Jose Vasquez, Director
Hunter College and The Research Foundation
  of the City University of New York
695 Park Ave., Box 367
New York, NY 10021
(212) 772-4764

Service Area 3: Delaware, District of Columbia, Kentucky, Maryland, New Jersey, Pennsylvania, Ohio, Virginia, West Virginia

Mai Tran, Director
COMSIS, Corp.
8737 Colesville Rd., Suite 1100
Silver Spring, MD 20910
(301) 588-0800
(800) 228-6723

Service Area 4: Alabama, Florida, Georgia, Mississippi, North Carolina, South Carolina, Tennessee

Ann Willig, Director
Florida Atlantic University
College of Education
500 N.W. 20th St.
Boca Raton, FL 33431
(407) 388-1615

Service Area 5: Arkansas, Illinois, Indiana, Louisiana, Missouri

Minerva Coyne, Director
InterAmerican Research Associates
2360 East Devon Ave., Suite 3011
Des Plaines, IL 60018
(708) 296-6070

Service Area 6: Iowa, Michigan, Minnesota, Wisconsin

Walter Secada, Director
Wisconsin Center for Education Research
University of Wisconsin, Madison
1025 West Johnson St.
Madison, WI 53706
(608) 263-4216

Service Area 7: Texas

Betty J. Mace Matluck, Director
Southwest Educational Development Lab
211 East 7th St.
Austin, TX 78701
(512) 476-6861

Service Area 8: Oklahoma, Kansas, Nebraska, North Dakota, South Dakota

Hai Tran, Director
University of Oklahoma
Division of Continuing Education
  and Public Affairs
555 Constitution Ave.
Norman, OK 73037
(405) 325-1731

Service Area 9: Idaho, Montana, Oregon, Washington, Wyoming

Esther Puentes, Director
Interface Network, Inc.
4800 S. W. Griffith Dr., Suite 202
Beaverton, OR 97005
(503) 644-5741

Service Area 10: Arizona, Colorado, Nevada, New Mexico, Utah

Director: Rudy Chavez
Arizona State University, AMR/0208
College of Education
Tempe, AZ 85287
(602) 965-5688

Service Area 11: Southern California

Ruben Espinsora, Director
San Diego State University Foundation
6363 Alvarado Court, Suite 200
San Diego, CA 92120
(619) 594-5193

Service Area 12: Northern California

Sau-Lim Tsang, Director
ARC Associates, Inc.
310 Eighth St., Suite 311
Oakland, CA 94607
(415) 834-9455

Service Area 13: Puerto Rico, Virgin Islands

Cesar Cruz Cabello, Director
Metropolitan University
Apartado 21150
Rio Piedras, PR 00928
(809) 766-1717

Service Area 14: Hawaii, American Samoa

Winona Change, Director
ARC Associates, Inc.
1314 South King St., Suite 1456
Honolulu, HI 96814

Service Area 15: Guam, Commonwealth of the Northern Marianas, Federated States of Micronesia, Republic of the Marshall Islands, Republic of Palau, Wake Islands

Director: Mary Spencer
University of Guam
Project BEAM, College of Education
UOG Station
Mingilao, Guam 96913
(671) 734-4113

Service Area 16: Alaska

Richard Littlebear, Director
Interface Network, Inc.
3650 Lake Otis Parkway, Suite 102
Anchorage, AK 99501

Index

H

Historical perspectives, 3–4
Home language surveys, 13–14

I

Immersion, 4–5
Immersion programs, 24
    structured immersion, 25
    two-way immersion, 25–26
Immersion vs. submersion, 25
Immigrants
    rights of, 66–67
Intermediate learners
    approaches for, 38

K

Know-Nothing movement, 67
Krashen, Stephen, 36

L

Language acquistion vs. language learning, 36
Language Assessment Scales (LAS), 17-18
Language elitism, 10
Language parochialism, 9–10
Language policy, 1–3
Language proficiency
    definitions of, 14–15
    evaluating, 16
    Language Assessment Scales, 17-18
    of teachers, 43–44
    testing, 16–19
Language restrictionism, 10–11
Language-minority students
    identifying, 13–14
    number in United States, 14
Latin, 4
Lau v. Nichols, 8–9, 54–55
LEP students
    See Limited-English-proficient students
Limited-English-proficient students
    identifying, 13–14
    number in California, 53
    number in Massachusetts, 52
    number in New Jersey, 52
    number in Texas, 53
    number in United States, 14, 52
Linguistic theory, 44-45
    See also Second-language acquisition theory

two-way programs, 24

Q

Questions
 effective use of, 63

R

Rationale for bilingual instruction, 11–12
Reading, 39–40
Removing students from bilingual classrooms, 65
Rights of LEP students, 53–58

S

Second-language acquisition theory, 35–36
 See also Linguistic theory
Second-language instruction, 34–35
Self-esteem, 22
Sheltered English, 38
Social and affective learning strategies, 39
Sociocultural issues, 46–47
Sociolinguistic competence, 15
Soviet Union
 language restrictionism in, 10
Spanish, 5
St. Lambert experiment, 4
State law and bilingual education, 56
 Chacon-Moscone Bilingual-Bicultural Education Act, 57
 Florida Consent Decree, 57–58
Strategic competence, 15
Structured immersion programs, 25
Submersion programs, 25
Subsystems of language, 16–17
Subtractive bilingualism, 22
Swain, M., 15

T

Teacher competencies, 43
Teacher qualifications, 42–47, 49
Teaching strategies, 62–63
Testing language proficiency, 16–19
Title VII of ESEA
 See Bilingual Education Act
Transitional programs, 23
Two-way immersion programs, 25–26
Two-way programs, 24

U

U.S. English, 67
Undocumented students
  rights of, 66–67
United States
  official language policy in, 67–68
United States Department of Education, 65
  longitudinal study from, 28
United States history
  European immigrant languages, 6
  German example, 5–6
  Native American languages, 6
  nativism, 7
  World War II and beyond, 7

V

Voting Rights Act of 1965, 11

W

World War II
  influence on second-language instruction, 7, 35